*~ All Time ~*

# FAMILY FAVORITES™

# COUNTRY BAKING

## BREADS, MUFFINS & MORE

PUBLICATIONS INTERNATIONAL, LTD.

**Microwave Cooking:** Microwave ovens may vary in wattage. The microwave cooking times given in the publication are approximate. Use the cooking times as guidelines and check for doneness before adding more time. Consult manufacturer's instructions for suitable microwave-safe dishes.

# — Contents —

Introduction 4

Sensational Morning Glories 6

Tasty Team-Ups 34

Terrific Light Delights 72

Sweet Snackin' Treats 92

Acknowledgments 124

Index 125

# Introduction

No one can resist the homemade flavor of a fresh-baked slice of banana bread smothered with jelly, a moist and tender muffin oozing with chocolatey goodness or a hot, billowy popover lavished with butter. If you always thought baking bread was too complicated and time-consuming, read on. Your homemade breads will add new life to soups and salads, transform ordinary sandwiches into taste sensations and turn breakfast into a meal that can't be missed. To ensure the best possible results, read the following information to familiarize yourself with the bread-making methods.

## Muffins and Quick Loaves

When making muffins and other quick breads, start by combining the dry ingredients in a large bowl. This is done to distribute the baking powder and/or baking soda with the flour. Then, the liquid ingredients are combined in a separate bowl and stirred into the dry ingredients just until the dry ingredients are moistened. The batter will still be lumpy. Overstirring the batter develops the gluten in the flour and causes the baked muffins to have tunnels, peaked tops and a tough texture. Finally, nuts, fruits, chocolate chips or other ingredients are gently folded into the batter.

For muffins, always grease or paper-line muffin cups prior to filling. If a recipe does not call for foil or paper liners, grease the muffin cups since that particular batter will stick to the liners when baked. When making jumbo muffins, be sure to grease the top surface of the muffin pan to prevent the batter from sticking. Unless otherwise stated, muffin cups should be filled two-thirds to three-quarters full with batter. When adding batter to the pan, a ¼-cup measure or a soup ladle is less messy than a spoon and makes it easier to place an equal amount of batter in each cup. If there is not enough batter to fill all of the cups, fill the empty cups half full with water to prevent the pan from scorching or warping in the oven. The water also allows for even baking. Begin checking for doneness at the minimum time given in the recipe. Quick breads are done when the center springs back when lightly touched and, in most cases, when a wooden pick inserted in the center comes out clean.

Store cooled muffins and quick breads at room temperature in a sealed plastic food storage bag up to three days or wrap them in heavy-duty foil and store for up to one month in the freezer. To reheat, warm in a preheated 350°F oven for about 20 minutes or unwrap and microwave on High for about 45 seconds per muffin or slice of bread.

## Biscuits and Scones

When making these quick breads, butter or shortening is cut into the dry ingredients with a pastry blender or two knives until the mixture forms coarse crumbs. Further blending of the fat produces a mealy texture. Add the combined liquid ingredients and mix into the dough gently and quickly; overworking the dough makes the biscuits or scones tough. These doughs may be kneaded very briefly to bring the dough together to be shaped. When cutting biscuits, press a floured cutter straight down through the dough. Avoid twisting the cutter as it may produce a lopsided biscuit. Biscuits and scones are finished baking when the bottom and top crusts are evenly and lightly browned.

## Popovers

Popover pan cups or custard cups should be generously greased to insure the easy removal and rising of popovers. Just before filling the cups, stir the batter since it will have settled after mixing. To prevent overbrowning, lower the oven shelf so the tops of the popover pan cups or custard cups are in the center of the oven. Popovers are done when they are firm to the touch and the tops are golden brown. Since popovers will fall if they are underdone, follow baking times carefully and bake until they are firm. Do not open the oven while baking since the rush of cool air can make them fall. For crisp popovers, turn the oven off after they test done and let the popovers stand in the hot oven 5 minutes longer or to desired crispness. To prevent popovers from becoming soggy, prick them with a fork immediately after removing from oven. This allows the steam to escape. Remove popovers from the pans while they are still warm. Popovers are best when served hot.

## Yeast Breads

Yeast breads contain yeast as a leavening agent. They require stirring or kneading to develop the gluten that gives the bread its structure. Yeast dough breads are kneaded to develop the gluten, producing breads with a chewy texture and good volume. These doughs become smooth and elastic with kneading. Sweet yeast doughs are softer and stickier than regular yeast doughs because they contain more sweeteners and fat.

**Kneading the dough:** Kneading is essential to develop and strengthen the gluten that forms the internal structure of the bread. Kneading also incorporates and homogenizes the ingredients in the dough. The dough will be sticky after all the ingredients are mixed in, gradually becoming smoother, elastic and less sticky as it is kneaded. Bread dough may be kneaded by hand; an electric mixer with a dough hook attachment or a food processor may also be used to mix and knead doughs quickly and efficiently.

To knead dough by hand, flour the kneading surface and your hands lightly before beginning in order to make the dough easier to handle. Flatten the dough slightly and fold it in half toward you. Press the dough away from you with the heels of your hands in a rolling motion. Rotate the dough one-quarter turn and repeat the folding, pushing and turning steps for the length of time specified by each recipe. Kneading times will vary with the dough. For example, biscuit doughs only require a few gentle strokes while most yeast bread doughs are kneaded vigorously for 5 to 10 minutes. Follow specific recipe directions.

**Rising:** Letting the dough rise means allowing time for the yeast cells to give off carbon dioxide gas. This process gradually expands and develops the dough, in flavor and texture as well as structure. To prevent the kneaded dough from drying out and developing a crust, place the dough in a greased bowl and turn it over so the top is also greased. Cover the dough or batter with a clean kitchen towel and set in a warm place (80° to 85°F) away from drafts until it has doubled or almost doubled in bulk. Use the time guidelines given in each recipe. Cold temperatures cause batters and doughs to rise slowly, offering the convenience of beginning a recipe one day and completing it later that day or the next day. For the refrigerator rising method, batters and doughs are covered with plastic wrap and set in the refrigerator to rise for 3 to 24 hours. They are then brought to room temperature and shaped or baked as specified in the recipe. To test if the dough has risen enough, lightly press two fingertips about one-half inch into the dough. The dough is ready if the indentations remain when fingertips are removed.

# MORNING GLORIES

## COUNTRY BISCUITS

**2 cups all-purpose flour**
**1 tablespoon baking powder**
**1 teaspoon salt**
**⅓ CRISCO® Stick or ⅓ cup CRISCO**
**all-vegetable shortening**
**¾ cup milk**

1. **Preheat** oven to 425°F. **Combine** flour, baking powder and salt in medium bowl. **Cut** in shortening using pastry blender (or two knives) to form coarse crumbs. **Add** milk. **Mix** with fork until dry mixture is moistened. **Form** dough into a ball.

2. **Transfer** dough to lightly floured surface. **Knead** gently 8 to 10 times. **Roll** dough ½ inch thick. **Cut** with floured 2-inch round cutter. **Place** on ungreased baking sheet.

3. **Bake** at 425°F. 12 to 14 minutes or until golden. Serve warm.

*Makes 12 to 16 biscuits*

## MORNING GLORIES

## APPLE BUTTER SPICE MUFFINS

½ cup sugar
1 teaspoon ground cinnamon
¼ teaspoon ground nutmeg
⅛ teaspoon ground allspice
½ cup pecans or walnuts, chopped
2 cups all-purpose flour
2 teaspoons baking powder
¼ teaspoon salt
1 cup milk
¼ cup vegetable oil
1 egg
¼ cup apple butter

Preheat oven to 400°F. Grease or paper-line 12 (2½-inch) muffin cups; set aside.

Combine sugar, cinnamon, nutmeg and allspice in large bowl. Toss 2 tablespoons sugar mixture with pecans in small bowl; set aside. Add flour, baking powder and salt to remaining sugar mixture. Combine milk, oil and egg in medium bowl until well blended; stir into flour mixture just until moistened. Spoon 1 tablespoon batter into each prepared muffin cup. Spoon 1 teaspoon apple butter into each cup. Spoon remaining batter over apple butter. Sprinkle reserved pecan mixture over top of each muffin.

Bake 20 to 25 minutes or until golden brown and wooden pick inserted in center comes out clean. Remove from pan. Cool on wire rack 10 minutes.

*Makes 12 muffins*

## BUTTERMILK OATMEAL SCONES

2 cups all-purpose flour, sifted
1 cup uncooked rolled oats
⅓ cup granulated sugar
1 tablespoon baking powder
½ teaspoon baking soda
⅛ teaspoon salt
6 tablespoons cold unsalted margarine, cut into small pieces
1 cup buttermilk

Preheat oven to 375°F. Grease baking sheets; set aside.

Combine flour, oats, sugar, baking powder, baking soda and salt in large bowl. Cut in margarine with pastry blender or process in food processor until mixture resembles coarse crumbs. Add buttermilk; stir with fork until soft dough forms. Turn out dough onto lightly floured surface; knead 10 to 12 times. Roll out dough to ½-inch-thick rectangle with lightly floured rolling pin. Cut dough into circles with lightly floured 1½-inch biscuit cutter. Place on prepared baking sheets. Brush tops with buttermilk and sprinkle with sugar. Bake 18 to 20 minutes or until golden brown and wooden pick inserted in center comes out clean. Remove from baking sheets. Cool on wire racks 10 minutes. Serve warm or cool completely.

*Makes about 30 scones*

*Favorite recipe from **The Sugar Association, Inc.***

*Apple Butter Spice Muffins*

## MORNING GLORIES

## CINNAMON BUNS

**1 recipe Sweet Yeast Dough (page 12)**
**½ cup granulated sugar**
**2 teaspoons ground cinnamon**
**2 tablespoons butter or margarine, melted**
**½ cup raisins, divided (optional)**
**2 cups sifted powdered sugar**
**2 tablespoons milk**
**½ teaspoon vanilla**

Prepare Sweet Yeast Dough; let rise as directed.

Combine granulated sugar and cinnamon in small bowl; set aside. Grease two 9-inch round cake pans. Divide dough in half. Roll half of dough into 12×8-inch rectangle on lightly floured surface with lightly floured rolling pin. Brush rectangle with half of melted butter; sprinkle with half of sugar mixture and half of raisins, if desired. Starting with 1 (12-inch) side, roll up jelly-roll fashion. (Do not roll dough too tightly because centers of rolls will pop up as they rise.) Repeat with remaining dough, butter, sugar mixture and raisins.

Cut each roll into 12 (1-inch) slices with floured sharp knife or dental floss. (To use dental floss, position under roll; bring up ends, cross over center and gently pull floss to cut each slice.)

Place slices ½ inch apart in prepared pans. Rolls will spread as they rise. Cover with towel; let rise in warm place about 1 hour or until doubled in bulk.

Preheat oven to 350°F. Bake 20 to 25 minutes or until rolls are golden brown. Cool in pans on wire racks 10 minutes.

Combine powdered sugar, milk and vanilla in small bowl until smooth. Spread mixture over rolls. Serve warm. *Makes 24 buns*

## ORANGE–ALMOND MUFFINS

**2 tablespoons butter or margarine**
**¼ cup packed brown sugar**
**½ cup BLUE DIAMOND® Blanched Slivered Almonds, toasted**
**½ package (14 ounces) orange muffin mix**
**¼ cup orange juice**

Beat butter and sugar in small bowl until creamy; gently stir in almonds. Spoon evenly into 6 to 8 well-greased muffin cups, filling each about two-thirds full. Prepare muffin mix as package directs, substituting orange juice for water. Spoon evenly into muffin cups.

Bake as package directs. Remove from pan. Cool on wire rack 10 minutes. Serve warm or cool completely. *Makes 6 to 8 muffins*

**ALMOND BLUEBERRY MUFFINS:**
Substitute blueberry muffin mix for orange muffin mix. Continue as directed.

*Cinnamon Buns*

# MORNING GLORIES

## SWEET YEAST DOUGH

   **4 to 4¼ cups all-purpose flour, divided**
**½ cup sugar**
   **2 packages active dry yeast**
   **1 teaspoon salt**
**¾ cup milk**
   **4 tablespoons butter or margarine**
   **2 eggs**
   **1 teaspoon vanilla**

Combine 1 cup flour, sugar, yeast and salt in large bowl; set aside.

Combine milk and butter in 1-quart saucepan. Heat over low heat until mixture is 120° to 130°F. (Butter does not need to completely melt.) Gradually beat milk mixture into flour mixture with electric mixer at low speed. Increase speed to medium; beat 2 minutes. Reduce speed to low. Beat in eggs, vanilla and 1 cup flour. Increase speed to medium; beat 2 minutes. Stir in enough additional flour, about 2 cups, with wooden spoon to make soft dough.

Turn out dough onto lightly floured surface; flatten slightly. Knead dough about 5 minutes or until smooth and elastic, adding ¼ cup more flour to prevent sticking if necessary. Shape dough into a ball; place in large greased bowl. Turn dough over so that top is greased. Cover with towel; let rise in warm place 1½ to 2 hours or until doubled in bulk.

Punch down dough. Knead dough on lightly floured surface 1 minute. Cover with towel; let rest 10 minutes.

**NOTE:** This dough is used to make Cinnamon Buns (page 10) and Maple Nut Twist (page 22).

**REFRIGERATOR SWEET YEAST DOUGH:** Prepare Sweet Yeast Dough. Shape dough into a ball; place in large greased bowl. Turn dough over so that top is greased. Cover with plastic wrap; refrigerate 3 to 24 hours. Punch down dough. Knead dough on lightly floured surface 1 to 2 minutes. Cover with towel; let dough rest 20 minutes before shaping and second rising. (Second rising may take up to 1½ hours.)

## GOLDEN APPLE CHEESE MUFFINS

   **1 or 2 (about 6 ounces each) Washington Golden Delicious apples, cored and sliced**
   **2 tablespoons butter or margarine**
**½ cup creamed cottage cheese**
   **2 tablespoons sugar**
   **1 teaspoon instant minced onion**
   **1 egg**
   **2 cups buttermilk baking mix**

**FOOD PROCESSOR METHOD:** Place apples in bowl of food processor; chop with steel blade to measure 1½ cups. Combine apples and butter; cook, covered, several minutes or until tender. Cool

slightly. With steel blade in bowl of food processor, process cottage cheese, sugar and onion. Add egg; process until smooth. Add apple mixture to cheese mixture and process thoroughly. Add baking mix; process only to mix. *Do not over process.* Spoon into well-greased muffin pan.\* Bake at 400°F. 25 to 30 minutes. *Makes 12 muffins*

\*Muffin pan will be very full.

**CONVENTIONAL METHOD:** Finely chop apples by hand to measure 1½ cups. Combine apples and butter; cook, covered, several minutes or until tender. Cream cottage cheese, sugar and onion in small bowl of electric mixer. Add egg; mix well. Add apple mixture to cheese mixture and beat thoroughly. Stir in baking mix with spoon; stir only until mixed. Bake as above.

**FREEZER TIP:** Muffins can be frozen. Wrap securely in foil or freezer wrap. Best if used within 2 weeks.

*Favorite recipe from **Washington Apple Commission***

## WHEAT GERM SCONES

   ½ **cup wheat germ, divided**
1½ **cups all-purpose flour**
   2 **tablespoons packed brown sugar**
   1 **tablespoon baking powder**
   ½ **teaspoon salt**
   6 **tablespoons butter or margarine**
   ⅓ **cup golden raisins, coarsely chopped**
   2 **eggs**
   ¼ **cup milk**

Preheat oven to 425°F.

Reserve 1 tablespoon wheat germ. Combine remaining wheat germ, flour, brown sugar, baking powder and salt in large bowl. Cut in butter with pastry blender or 2 knives until mixture resembles coarse crumbs. Stir in raisins. Beat eggs in small bowl. Add milk; beat until well blended. Reserve 2 tablespoons milk mixture. Add remaining milk mixture to flour mixture; stir until mixture forms soft dough that pulls away from side of bowl.

Turn out dough onto well-floured surface. Knead dough 10 times.\* Roll out dough with lightly floured rolling pin into 9×6-inch rectangle. Cut dough into 6 (3-inch) squares with lightly floured knife. Cut each square diagonally in half, making 12 triangles. Place triangles 2 inches apart on *ungreased* baking sheets. Brush triangles with reserved milk mixture; sprinkle with reserved wheat germ.

Bake 10 to 12 minutes or until golden brown. Cool on wire racks 10 minutes. Serve warm or cool completely. *Makes 12 scones*

\*To knead dough, fold dough in half toward you and press dough away from you with heels of hands. Give dough a quarter turn and continue folding, pressing and turning.

## HOT CROSS BUNS

**4½ to 5 cups all-purpose flour**
**½ cup granulated sugar**
**2 packages active dry yeast**
**1 teaspoon salt**
**1½ cups plus 1 tablespoon milk, divided**
**½ cup butter or margarine**
**3 eggs, divided**
**1 cup raisins**
**1 tablespoon water**
**¾ cup sifted powdered sugar**
**½ teaspoon vanilla**

Combine 2 cups all-purpose flour, granulated sugar, yeast and salt in large bowl.

Combine 1½ cups milk and butter in 1-quart saucepan. Heat over low heat until mixture is 120° to 130°F. (Butter does not need to completely melt.) Gradually beat milk mixture into flour mixture with electric mixer at low speed. Increase speed to medium; beat 2 minutes. Reduce speed to low. Beat in 2 eggs and 1½ cups all-purpose flour. Increase speed to medium; beat 2 minutes. Stir in raisins and enough remaining all-purpose flour, about 1 cup, with wooden spoon to make soft dough.

Turn out dough onto lightly floured surface; flatten slightly. Knead dough 8 to 10 minutes or until smooth and elastic, adding ½ cup more all-purpose flour to prevent sticking if necessary.

Shape dough into a ball. Place in large greased bowl. Turn dough over so that top is greased. Cover with towel. Let rise in warm place about 1 hour or until doubled in bulk.

Punch down dough. Knead dough on lightly floured surface 1 minute. Cut dough in half. Cover with towel; let rest 10 minutes.

Grease 2 (8×8-inch) square baking pans or 1 (13×9-inch) baking pan. Divide dough into 18 pieces. Shape each piece into a ball. Place balls in rows in prepared pans. Cover with towel; let rise in warm place about 45 minutes or until doubled in bulk.

Preheat oven to 350°F. Beat remaining egg and 1 tablespoon water in small bowl. Cut a cross in top of each bun with tip of sharp knife. Brush rolls with egg mixture.

Bake 20 to 25 minutes or until buns are golden brown and sound hollow when tapped. Immediately remove from pans. Cool on wire racks while preparing icing.

To make icing, combine powdered sugar, vanilla and remaining 1 tablespoon milk in small bowl until smooth. Spoon into decorating bag fitted with medium writing tip (#8). If using disposable decorating bag, cut pointed end so that opening is about ¼ inch wide. Fill cross in each bun with icing.

*Makes 18 servings*

*Hot Cross Buns*

## APRICOT SCONES

**1½ cups all-purpose flour**
**1 cup oat bran**
**2 tablespoons sugar**
**1 tablespoon baking powder**
**½ teaspoon salt**
**½ cup margarine**
**1 egg, beaten**
**3 tablespoons low fat milk**
**1 can (17 ounces) California apricot halves,**
**drained and chopped**

Preheat oven to 400°F.

Combine flour, oat bran, sugar, baking powder and salt in large bowl. Cut in margarine with pastry blender or 2 knives until mixture resembles fine crumbs. Add egg, milk and apricots; stir just until dough leaves side of bowl.

Divide dough in half; place on lightly floured surface. Sprinkle surface of dough with additional flour. Roll or pat dough into 6-inch circle, 1 inch thick. Repeat with remaining dough. Cut each circle into six wedges with lightly floured knife. Place on *ungreased* baking sheet.

Bake 12 minutes or until golden brown and wooden pick inserted in center comes out clean. Remove from baking sheet. Cool on wire rack 10 minutes. Serve warm or cool completely.

*Makes 12 scones*

*Favorite recipe from* **California Apricot Advisory Board**

## FRESH NECTARINE MUFFINS

**1½ cups all-purpose flour**
**¾ cup toasted wheat germ**
**¼ cup sugar**
**1 tablespoon baking powder**
**1 teaspoon ground cinnamon**
**½ teaspoon salt**
**1½ fresh California nectarines, chopped**
**(1 cup)**
**½ cup low fat milk**
**½ cup raisins**
**¼ cup margarine, melted**
**1 egg**
**1 teaspoon grated lemon peel**

Preheat oven to 450°F. Grease 12 (2½-inch) muffin cups; set aside.

Combine flour, wheat germ, sugar, baking powder, cinnamon and salt in large bowl. Beat nectarines, milk, raisins, margarine, egg and lemon peel in medium bowl with electric mixer at medium speed until well blended. Stir into flour mixture just until moistened. Spoon evenly into prepared muffin cups.

Bake 15 minutes or until golden brown and wooden pick inserted in center comes out clean. Remove from pan. Cool on wire rack 10 minutes. Serve warm or cool completely.

*Makes 12 muffins*

*Favorite recipe from* **California Tree Fruit Agreement**

*Apricot Scones*

MORNING GLORIES

## CINNAMON–DATE SCONES

¼ **cup sugar, divided**
¼ **teaspoon ground cinnamon**
2 **cups all-purpose flour**
2½ **teaspoons baking powder**
½ **teaspoon salt**
5 **tablespoons cold butter or margarine**
½ **cup chopped pitted dates**
2 **eggs**
⅓ **cup half-and-half or milk**

1. Preheat oven to 425°F.

2. Combine 2 tablespoons sugar and cinnamon in small bowl; set aside. Combine flour, baking powder, salt and remaining 2 tablespoons sugar in medium bowl. Cut in butter with pastry blender or 2 knives until mixture resembles coarse crumbs. Stir in dates.

3. Beat eggs in separate small bowl with fork. Add half-and-half; beat until well blended. Reserve 1 tablespoon egg mixture in small cup; set aside. Stir remaining egg mixture into flour mixture until soft dough forms.

4. Turn out dough onto well-floured surface. Knead dough gently 10 to 12 times.

5. Roll out dough with lightly floured rolling pin into 9×6-inch rectangle.

6. Cut dough into 6 (3-inch) squares with lightly floured knife. Cut each square diagonally in half, making 12 triangles.

7. Place triangles 2 inches apart on *ungreased* baking sheets. Brush triangles with reserved egg mixture; sprinkle with reserved sugar mixture.

8. Bake 10 to 12 minutes or until golden brown. Immediately remove from baking sheets. Cool on wire racks 10 minutes. Serve warm or cool completely.      *Makes 12 scones*

## BANANA–HONEY MUFFINS

1½ **cups oat bran flakes cereal**
1 **cup mashed ripe bananas (about**
     2 **medium)**
¾ **cup milk**
¼ **cup butter, melted**
1 **egg, beaten**
2 **tablespoons honey**
1¼ **cups all-purpose flour**
1 **tablespoon baking powder**
¼ **teaspoon salt**

Preheat oven to 400°F. Grease or paper-line 12 (2½-inch) muffin cups; set aside. Combine cereal, bananas, milk, butter, egg and honey in medium bowl. Let stand 5 minutes. Combine flour, baking powder and salt in large bowl. Add cereal mixture to flour mixture, stirring just until moistened. Spoon evenly into prepared muffin cups.

Bake 20 to 25 minutes or until wooden pick inserted in center comes out clean. Remove from pan. Cool on wire rack 10 minutes. Serve warm or cool completely.      *Makes 12 muffins*

*Cinnamon–Date Scones*

## MORNING GLORIES

## PINEAPPLE–RAISIN MUFFINS

¼ **cup finely chopped pecans**
¼ **cup packed light brown sugar**
2 **cups all-purpose flour**
¼ **cup granulated sugar**
2½ **teaspoons baking powder**
¾ **teaspoon salt**
½ **teaspoon ground cinnamon**
6 **tablespoons cold butter or margarine**
½ **cup raisins**
1 **can (8 ounces) crushed pineapple in juice, undrained**
⅓ **cup unsweetened pineapple juice**
1 **egg**

1. Preheat oven to 400°F. Grease or paper-line 12 (2½-inch) muffin cups; set aside.

2. Combine pecans and brown sugar in small bowl; set aside.

3. Combine flour, granulated sugar, baking powder, salt and cinnamon in large bowl. Cut in butter with pastry blender or 2 knives until mixture resembles fine crumbs. Stir in raisins.

4. Combine undrained pineapple, pineapple juice and egg in small bowl until blended; stir into flour mixture just until moistened.

5. Spoon evenly into prepared muffin cups, filling two-thirds full. Sprinkle with reserved pecan mixture.

6. Bake 20 to 25 minutes or until golden brown and wooden pick inserted in center comes out clean. Remove from pan. Cool on wire rack 10 minutes. Serve warm or cool completely.

*Makes 12 muffins*

## FIVE-FRUIT GRANOLA SCONES

2 **cups all-purpose flour**
⅓ **cup sugar, divided**
1 **tablespoon baking powder**
½ **teaspoon salt**
¼ **cup butter or margarine**
1 **cup granola**
1 **can (16 ounces) California fruit cocktail in juice or extra light syrup, drained**
2 **eggs, beaten**

Preheat oven to 375°F. Grease baking sheet; set aside. Combine flour, ¼ cup sugar, baking powder and salt in large bowl. Cut in butter with pastry blender or 2 knives until mixture resembles coarse crumbs; stir in granola. Stir in fruit cocktail and eggs; blend just until moistened. Place dough on lightly floured surface. Roll out dough into 7-inch circle with lightly floured rolling pin; place on prepared baking sheet. Sprinkle remaining sugar over top of dough. Bake 45 minutes or until wooden pick inserted in center comes out clean. Cut into 6 wedges. Remove from baking sheet. Cool on wire rack 10 minutes.    *Makes 6 scones*

*Favorite recipe from* **Canned Fruit Promotion Service**

*Pineapple-Raisin Muffins*

# MAPLE NUT TWIST

**1 recipe Sweet Yeast Dough (page 12)**
**2 tablespoons butter or margarine, melted**
**2 tablespoons honey**
**½ cup chopped pecans**
**¼ cup granulated sugar**
**2½ teaspoons maple extract, divided**
**½ teaspoon ground cinnamon**
**1 cup sifted powdered sugar**
**5 teaspoons milk**

Prepare Sweet Yeast Dough; let rise as directed. Combine butter and honey in custard cup; set aside. Combine pecans, granulated sugar, 2 teaspoons maple extract and cinnamon in small bowl. Toss to coat; set aside.

Grease 2 baking sheets; set aside. Cut dough in half; cut half of dough into 2 pieces. Roll out 1 piece dough into 9-inch circle on lightly floured surface with lightly floured rolling pin. (Keep remaining dough covered with towel.) Place on prepared baking sheet. Brush half of butter mixture over dough. Sprinkle half of pecan mixture over butter.

Roll remaining piece dough into 9-inch circle. Place rolling pin on one side of dough. Gently roll dough over rolling pin once. Carefully lift rolling pin and dough, unrolling dough over pecan filling, stretching dough as necessary to cover. Pinch edges to seal. Place 1-inch biscuit cutter* in center of circle as cutting guide, being careful not to cut through dough. Cut dough into 12 wedges with scissors or sharp knife, from edge of circle to edge of biscuit cutter, cutting through all layers. Pick up wide edge of 1 wedge, twist several times and lay back down on prepared sheet. Repeat twisting procedure with remaining 11 wedges. Repeat with remaining half of dough, butter mixture and pecan mixture. Cover coffee cakes with towel. Let rise in warm place about 1 hour or until doubled in bulk.

Preheat oven to 350°F. Bake on 2 racks in oven 20 to 25 minutes or until coffee cakes are golden brown and sound hollow when tapped. (Rotate baking sheets top to bottom halfway through baking.) Immediately remove from baking sheets; cool on wire racks about 30 minutes.

Combine powdered sugar, milk and remaining ½ teaspoon maple extract in small bowl until smooth. Drizzle over warm coffee cakes.

*Makes 24 servings (2 coffee cakes)*

*Or, use the lid of an herb jar if biscuit cutter is not available.

*Maple Nut Twist*

**MORNING GLORIES**

## ALMOND BANANA BREAD

**2 cups ripe banana purée (about 4 large bananas)**
**½ cup granulated sugar**
**½ cup packed light brown sugar**
**½ cup vegetable oil**
**3 eggs**
**1 teaspoon vanilla**
**2 cups all-purpose flour**
**1 teaspoon baking soda**
**½ teaspoon baking powder**
**½ teaspoon salt**
**1¼ cups BLUE DIAMOND® Chopped Natural Almonds, toasted, divided**

Preheat oven to 350°F. Beat together first 6 ingredients in large bowl; set aside. Combine next 4 ingredients in small bowl; stir into banana mixture just until moistened. Reserving 2 tablespoons almonds for top, stir remaining almonds into batter. Pour batter into 1 greased and floured 9×5×3-inch loaf pan or 2 greased and floured 8½×4½×2½-inch loaf pans; sprinkle each loaf with reserved almonds. Bake at 350°F. for 50 minutes or until toothpick inserted in center comes out clean. (If browning too quickly, cover tops loosely with foil.) Cool in pans 10 minutes; turn out onto wire rack and cool completely.

*Makes 1 large loaf or 2 small loaves*

## WILD RICE AND BLUEBERRY MUFFINS

**1½ cups all-purpose flour**
**½ cup sugar**
**2 teaspoons baking powder**
**1 teaspoon ground coriander**
**½ teaspoon salt**
**1 cup fresh blueberries**
**½ cup milk**
**¼ cup melted butter**
**2 eggs**
**½ cup cooked wild rice**

Preheat oven to 400°F. Grease 12 (2½-inch) muffin cups; set aside.

Combine flour, sugar, baking powder, coriander and salt in large bowl. Spoon 1 tablespoon flour mixture over blueberries in small bowl; toss to coat. Combine milk, butter and eggs in another small bowl until well blended; stir into flour mixture just until moistened. Fold blueberries and wild rice into flour mixture. (Batter will be stiff.) Spoon evenly into prepared muffin cups.

Bake 15 to 20 minutes or until wooden pick inserted in center comes out clean. Remove from pan. Cool on wire rack 10 minutes. Serve warm or cool completely.
*Makes 12 muffins*

*Favorite recipe from **Minnesota Cultivated Wild Rice Council***

## MORNING GLORIES

## NECTARINE PECAN BREAKFAST MUFFINS

1½ cups whole wheat flour
½ cup chopped pecans
¼ cup packed brown sugar
2 teaspoons baking powder
½ teaspoon salt
½ teaspoon ground nutmeg
1½ fresh California nectarines, chopped (1 cup)
1 cup low fat milk
1 egg, beaten
3 tablespoons vegetable oil
12 pecan halves for garnish

Preheat oven to 400°F. Grease 12 (2½-inch) muffin cups; set aside.

Combine flour, chopped pecans, sugar, baking powder, salt and nutmeg in large bowl.

Combine nectarines, milk, egg and oil in medium bowl until well blended. Stir into flour mixture just until moistened. (Batter will be thick and lumpy.) Spoon evenly into prepared muffin cups. Place pecan half on top of each muffin. Bake 20 minutes or until golden brown and wooden pick inserted in center comes out clean. Remove from pan. Cool on wire rack 10 minutes. Serve warm or cool completely. *Makes 12 muffins*

*Favorite recipe from **California Tree Fruit Agreement***

## SWEET HEARTLAND BISCUITS

1⅔ cups QUAKER® Oats (quick or old fashioned, uncooked), divided
1½ cups all-purpose flour
¼ cup firmly packed brown sugar
1 tablespoon plus 1 teaspoon baking powder
½ teaspoon baking soda
⅛ teaspoon salt (optional)
¼ CRISCO® stick or ¼ cup CRISCO all-vegetable shortening
1 cup low fat buttermilk

1. **Heat** oven to 450°F. **Reserve** ⅓ cup oats.

2. **Combine** 1⅓ cups oats, flour, brown sugar, baking powder, baking soda and salt, if used, in large bowl. **Cut** in shortening using pastry blender (or 2 knives) until coarse crumbs form. **Add** buttermilk. **Stir** with fork until dry ingredients are moistened and cling together. **Form** dough into ball.

3. **Transfer** dough to lightly floured surface. Knead 6 to 8 times. **Sprinkle** floured surface with half of reserved oats. **Roll** dough with floured rolling pin to ½-inch thickness. **Sprinkle** remaining oats on top of dough. **Cut** with floured 2½-inch round cutter. Place on *ungreased* baking sheet.

4. **Bake** at 450°F. for 12 to 14 minutes or until light golden brown. Serve warm.

*Makes 12 biscuits*

## CHERRY COCONUT CHEESE COFFEE CAKE

**2½ cups all-purpose flour**
**¾ cup sugar**
**½ teaspoon baking powder**
**½ teaspoon baking soda**
**2 packages (3 ounces each) cream cheese, softened, divided**
**¾ cup milk**
**2 tablespoons vegetable oil**
**2 eggs, divided**
**1 teaspoon vanilla**
**½ cup flaked coconut**
**¾ cup cherry preserves**
**2 tablespoons butter or margarine**

Preheat oven to 350°F. Grease and flour 9-inch springform pan.

Combine flour and sugar in large bowl. Reserve ½ cup flour mixture. Stir baking powder and baking soda into flour mixture in large bowl. Cut in 1 package cream cheese with pastry blender or 2 knives until mixture resembles coarse crumbs; set aside.

Combine milk, oil and 1 egg in medium bowl. Add to flour-cream cheese mixture; stir just until moistened. Spread batter on bottom and 1 inch up side of prepared pan. (Batter should be about ¼ inch thick on sides.) Combine remaining package cream cheese, remaining egg and vanilla in small bowl; stir until smooth. Pour over batter, spreading to within 1 inch of edge. Sprinkle coconut over cheese mixture. Spoon preserves evenly over coconut.

Cut butter into reserved flour mixture with pastry blender or 2 knives until mixture resembles coarse crumbs. Sprinkle over preserves.

Bake 55 to 60 minutes or until browned and toothpick inserted in coffee cake crust comes out clean. Cool in pan on wire rack 15 minutes. Remove side of pan. Serve warm or cool completely. *Makes 10 servings*

## GRAHAM MUFFINS

**2 Stay Fresh Packs HONEY MAID® Grahams, finely rolled (about 3 cups crumbs)**
**¼ cup sugar**
**1 tablespoon DAVIS® Baking Powder**
**2 eggs, well beaten**
**1½ cups milk**
**⅓ cup margarine, melted**

In medium bowl, combine crumbs, sugar and baking powder; set aside.

In small bowl, combine eggs, milk and margarine; stir into crumb mixture just until moistened. Spoon batter into 12 greased 2½-inch muffin-pan cups.

Bake at 400°F for 18 to 20 minutes or until toothpick inserted in center comes out clean. Serve warm. *Makes 1 dozen muffins*

*Cherry Coconut Cheese Coffee Cake*

## MORNING GLORIES

## APPLE RING COFFEE CAKE

**3 cups all-purpose flour**
**1 teaspoon baking soda**
**1 teaspoon salt**
**1 teaspoon ground cinnamon**
**1 cup chopped walnuts**
**1½ cups granulated sugar**
**1 cup vegetable oil**
**2 teaspoons vanilla**
**2 eggs**
**2 cups peeled chopped tart apples**
**Powdered sugar for garnish**

Preheat oven to 325°F. Grease 10-inch tube pan; set aside.

Sift together flour, baking soda, salt and cinnamon into large bowl. Stir in walnuts; set aside. Combine granulated sugar, oil, vanilla and eggs in medium bowl. Stir in apples. Stir into flour mixture just until moistened. Spoon batter into prepared pan, spreading evenly.

Bake 1 hour or until wooden toothpick inserted in center of cake comes out clean. Cool cake in pan on wire rack 10 minutes. Remove from pan; cool completely on wire rack. Sprinkle powdered sugar over cake. *Makes 12 servings*

## BANANA BREAKFAST MUFFINS

**1½ cups NABISCO® 100% Bran™**
**1 cup milk**
**¼ cup FLEISCHMANN'S® Margarine, melted**
**1 egg, slightly beaten**
**1 cup all-purpose flour**
**⅓ cup firmly packed light brown sugar**
**2 teaspoons DAVIS® Baking Powder**
**1 teaspoon ground cinnamon**
**½ cup mashed banana**
**½ cup seedless raisins**

Mix bran, milk, margarine and egg; let stand 5 minutes.

In bowl, blend flour, brown sugar, baking powder and cinnamon; stir in bran mixture just until blended. (Batter will be lumpy.)

Stir in banana and raisins. Spoon batter into 12 greased 2½-inch muffin-pan cups.

Bake at 400°F for 20 to 25 minutes or until toothpick inserted in center comes out clean. Serve warm. *Makes 1 dozen muffins*

**MICROWAVE DIRECTIONS:** Prepare batter as directed. In each of 6 microwavable muffin-pan cups, place 2 paper liners. Spoon batter into cups, filling ⅔ full. Microwave on HIGH (100% power) for 3 to 3½ minutes or until toothpick inserted in center comes out clean, rotating pan ½ turn after 2 minutes. Let stand in pan 5 minutes. Repeat with remaining batter. Serve warm.

*Apple Ring Coffee Cake*

MORNING GLORIES

## HONEY CURRANT SCONES

2½ **cups all-purpose flour**
2 **teaspoons grated orange peel**
1 **teaspoon baking powder**
½ **teaspoon baking soda**
½ **teaspoon salt**
½ **cup butter or margarine**
½ **cup currants**
½ **cup sour cream**
⅓ **cup honey**
1 **egg, slightly beaten**

Preheat oven to 375°F. Grease baking sheet; set aside.

Combine flour, orange peel, baking powder, baking soda and salt in large bowl. Cut in butter with pastry blender or 2 knives until mixture resembles coarse crumbs. Stir in currants. Combine sour cream, honey and egg in medium bowl until well blended. Stir into flour mixture until soft dough forms. Turn out dough onto lightly floured surface. Knead dough 10 times. Shape dough into 8-inch square. Cut into 4 squares; cut each square diagonally in half, making 8 triangles. Place triangles 1 inch apart on prepared baking sheet.

Bake 15 to 20 minutes or until golden brown and wooden pick inserted in center comes out clean. Remove from baking sheet. Cool on wire rack 10 minutes. Serve warm or cool completely.

*Makes 8 scones*

*Favorite recipe from* **National Honey Board**

## HEALTHY BANANA–WALNUT MUFFINS

2 **cups oat bran flakes cereal**
1½ **cups mashed ripe bananas (about 3 medium)**
½ **cup buttermilk**
¼ **cup butter, melted**
1 **egg**
1½ **cups all-purpose flour**
¼ **cup packed brown sugar**
1 **tablespoon baking powder**
½ **teaspoon ground cinnamon**
¼ **teaspoon baking soda**
¼ **cup chopped walnuts**

Preheat oven to 400°F. Grease or paper-line 12 (2½-inch) muffin cups; set aside.

Combine cereal, bananas, buttermilk, butter and egg in medium bowl. Let stand 5 minutes. Combine flour, brown sugar, baking powder, cinnamon and baking soda in large bowl. Add cereal mixture to flour mixture, stirring just until moistened. Spoon evenly into prepared muffin cups. Sprinkle with walnuts.

Bake 20 to 22 minutes or until wooden pick inserted in center comes out clean. Remove from pan. Cool on wire rack 10 minutes. Serve warm or cool completely.

*Makes 12 muffins*

**NOTE:** To freeze muffins, wrap tightly with foil or place in airtight container.

*Honey Currant Scones*

## APPLE SAUCY OATMEAL–RAISIN LOAF OR MUFFINS

**BREAD**
- ⅓ CRISCO® Stick or ⅓ cup CRISCO all-vegetable shortening
- ½ cup firmly packed brown sugar
- 4 egg whites
- 1 cup chunky applesauce
- 2 tablespoons water
- 1½ cups QUAKER® Oats (quick or old fashioned, uncooked)
- 1¼ cups all-purpose flour
- 1½ teaspoons cinnamon
- 1 teaspoon baking soda
- 1 teaspoon baking powder
- ¼ teaspoon salt (optional)
- 1 cup raisins

**TOPPING**
- 2 tablespoons QUAKER® Oats (quick or old fashioned, uncooked)
- 1½ teaspoons brown sugar
- ¼ teaspoon cinnamon
- 1 tablespoon chopped natural almonds

**GARNISH**
- Applesauce

**1. Heat** oven to 375°F. **Grease** 9×5×3-inch loaf pan.*

**2.** *For bread,* **combine** ⅓ cup shortening and ½ cup brown sugar in large bowl. **Beat** at medium speed of electric mixer or **stir** with fork until well blended. **Stir** in egg whites, 1 cup applesauce and water gradually.

**3. Combine** 1½ cups oats, flour, 1½ teaspoons cinnamon, baking soda, baking powder and salt, if used. **Stir** into liquid ingredients until just blended. **Stir** in raisins. **Spoon** into loaf pan.

**4.** *For topping,* **combine** 2 tablespoons oats, 1½ teaspoons brown sugar, ¼ teaspoon cinnamon and nuts. **Sprinkle** over top.

**5. Bake** at 375°F. for 50 to 60 minutes or until golden brown and toothpick inserted in center comes out clean. **Cool** 10 minutes in pan on rack. **Loosen** from sides. **Remove** from pan. **Cool** completely on rack.

**6. To serve, place** slice on serving plate. **Spoon** about 2 tablespoons additional applesauce over top of each slice.          *Makes 1 loaf (12 servings)*

*For muffins, heat oven to 400°F. **Line** 12 medium (about 2½-inch) muffin cups with foil or paper liners. **Fill** muffin cups almost full. **Sprinkle** with topping. **Bake** at 400°F. for 18 to 22 minutes or until golden brown and toothpick inserted in center comes out clean. **Cool** 5 minutes before removing from pan.          *Makes 12 muffins*

**NOTE:** Remaining applesauce can be spooned over muffin halves, if desired.

## MORNING GLORIES

## NECTARINE BRAN MUFFINS

1 cup natural high-fiber cereal
½ cup orange juice
1 cup all-purpose flour
¼ cup sugar
2½ teaspoons baking powder
½ teaspoon salt
¼ cup vegetable oil
1 egg
1½ fresh California nectarines, chopped
    (1 cup)

Preheat oven to 400°F. Grease 12 (2½-inch) muffin cups; set aside.

Combine cereal and orange juice in medium bowl; let stand 5 minutes or until cereal absorbs juice. Combine flour, sugar, baking powder and salt in large bowl; set aside. Stir oil and egg into cereal mixture until well blended. Stir into flour mixture with nectarines just until moistened. (Batter will be thick and lumpy.) Spoon evenly into prepared muffin cups.

Bake 25 minutes or until golden brown and wooden pick inserted in center comes out clean. Remove from pan. Cool on wire rack 10 minutes. Serve warm or cool completely.   *Makes 12 muffins*

*Favorite recipe from* **California Tree Fruit Agreement**

## APRICOT NUT BREAD

1½ cups coarsely chopped dried apricots
1 cup water
2½ cups all-purpose flour
¾ cup sugar
4 teaspoons baking powder
1 teaspoon salt
½ teaspoon baking soda
⅔ cup chopped nuts
1 egg, slightly beaten
1 cup buttermilk
3 tablespoons CRISCO® all-vegetable
    shortening, melted

1. **Heat** oven to 350°F. **Grease** bottom of 9×5×3-inch loaf pan.

2. **Combine** apricots and water in heavy saucepan. **Bring** to boiling. **Reduce** heat and **simmer,** uncovered, for 10 minutes or until water is absorbed. **Cool.**

3. **Combine** flour, sugar, baking powder, salt and baking soda in large bowl. **Stir** in nuts.

4. **Combine** apricots, egg, buttermilk and shortening. **Add** to dry ingredients. **Stir** only until dry ingredients are moistened.

5. **Turn** batter into prepared pan.

6. **Bake** at 350°F. for 55 to 60 minutes or until toothpick inserted in center comes out clean.

7. **Cool** for 10 minutes in pan on rack. **Remove** from pan; cool completely before slicing.

*Makes 1 loaf*

# — *Tasty* —

# TEAM-UPS

## WHOLE WHEAT POPOVERS

**2 eggs**
**1 cup milk**
**2 tablespoons butter or margarine, melted**
**½ cup all-purpose flour**
**½ cup whole wheat flour**
**¼ teaspoon salt**

Position rack in lower third of oven. Preheat oven to 450°F. Grease 6 (6-ounce) custard cups. Set custard cups in jelly-roll pan for easier handling; set aside.

Beat eggs in large bowl with electric mixer at low speed 1 minute. Beat in milk and butter until blended. Beat in flours and salt until batter is smooth. Pour evenly into prepared custard cups.

Bake 20 minutes. *Reduce oven temperature to 350°F.* Bake 15 minutes more; quickly make small slit in top of each popover to let out steam. Bake 5 to 10 minutes more or until browned. Remove from cups. Cool on wire rack 10 minutes. Serve warm or cool completely. *Makes 6 popovers*

TEAM-UPS

## THYME–CHEESE BUBBLE LOAF

- **1 package active dry yeast**
- **1 teaspoon sugar**
- **1 cup warm water (105° to 115°F)**
- **3 cups all-purpose flour**
- **1 teaspoon salt**
- **2 tablespoons vegetable oil**
- **1 cup (4 ounces) shredded Monterey Jack cheese**
- **4 tablespoons butter or margarine, melted**
- **¼ cup chopped fresh parsley**
- **3 teaspoons finely chopped fresh thyme *or* ¾ teaspoon dried thyme leaves, crushed**

To proof yeast, sprinkle yeast and sugar over warm water in small bowl; stir until yeast is dissolved. Let stand 5 minutes or until mixture is bubbly. Combine flour and salt in food processor.* With food processor running, add yeast mixture and oil through feed tube. Process until mixture forms dough that leaves side of food processor. If dough is too dry, add 1 to 2 tablespoons water. If dough is too wet, add 1 to 2 tablespoons additional flour until dough leaves side of bowl. Dough will be sticky. Place dough in large greased bowl. Turn dough over so that top is greased. Cover with towel; let rise in warm place about 1 hour or until doubled in bulk.

Punch down dough. Flour hands lightly. Knead cheese into dough on lightly floured surface until evenly distributed. Cover with towel; let rest 10 minutes.

Grease 8½×4½-inch loaf pan; set aside. Combine butter, parsley and thyme in small bowl. Roll out dough into 8×6-inch rectangle with lightly floured rolling pin. Cut dough into 48 squares with pizza cutter. Shape each square into a ball. Dip into parsley mixture. Place balls in prepared pan. Cover with towel; let rise in warm place about 45 minutes or until doubled in bulk.

Preheat oven to 375°F. Bake 35 to 40 minutes or until top is golden and loaf sounds hollow when tapped. Immediately remove from pan; cool on wire rack 30 minutes. Serve warm. Store leftover bread in refrigerator.  *Makes 1 loaf*

**\*TO PREPARE WITH ELECTRIC MIXER:**
Proof yeast as directed. Beat yeast mixture, 1½ cups flour, salt and oil in large bowl with electric mixer at low speed until blended, scraping down side of bowl once. Increase speed to medium; beat 2 minutes. Stir in enough additional flour, about 1 cup, to make soft dough. Turn out dough onto lightly floured surface; flatten slightly. Knead dough about 5 minutes or until smooth and elastic, adding ½ cup more flour to prevent sticking if necessary. Shape dough into a ball. Proceed as directed.

*Thyme-Cheese Bubble Loaf*

# TEAM-UPS

## SALSA MUFFINS

  1 cup all-purpose flour
  1 cup yellow cornmeal
  3 tablespoons sugar
  1 tablespoon baking powder
  ½ teaspoon salt
  6 tablespoons butter or margarine, softened
  ¾ cup bottled chunky salsa
  ½ cup milk
  1 egg

Preheat oven to 400°F. Grease or paper-line 12 (2½-inch) muffin cups; set aside.

Combine flour, cornmeal, sugar, baking powder and salt in large bowl. Cut in butter with pastry blender or 2 knives until mixture resembles fine crumbs. Combine salsa, milk and egg in small bowl until blended. Stir into flour mixture just until moistened. Spoon evenly into prepared muffin cups.

Bake 25 to 30 minutes or until golden brown and wooden pick inserted in center comes out clean. Remove from pan. Cool on wire rack 10 minutes. Serve warm or cool completely.

*Makes 12 muffins*

## CORNMEAL STICKS

  2 cups cold water
  1½ cups yellow cornmeal
  ¾ teaspoon salt
  6 ounces sharp Cheddar cheese, finely shredded (1½ cups)
  CRISCO® all-vegetable shortening for deep frying

**1. Combine** water, cornmeal and salt in a heavy saucepan. **Mix** until smooth. **Cook** over medium heat, stirring constantly, until mixture is very stiff, thick and pulls away from sides of pan. (This takes 6 to 9 minutes.)

**2. Remove** from heat. **Add** cheese. **Stir** until melted.

**3. Pat** mixture evenly into ungreased 13×9×2-inch baking dish. **Let** stand uncovered 30 minutes at room temperature. Do not chill dough.

**4. Cut** into 3 lengthwise sections and 18 crosswise strips.

**5. Heat** shortening to 365°F. in a deep saucepan or deep fryer.

**6. Add** sticks to hot shortening, 1 at a time, frying 3 sticks at a time for 3 minutes or until golden brown. (If sticks run together, cut apart after frying.) **Remove** with slotted spatula. **Drain** on paper towels. **Serve** warm.

*Makes 4½ dozen cornmeal sticks*

*Salsa Muffins*

## TEAM-UPS

## SWEET POTATO BISCUITS

**2½ cups all-purpose flour**
**¼ cup packed brown sugar**
**1 tablespoon baking powder**
**¾ teaspoon salt**
**¾ teaspoon ground cinnamon**
**¼ teaspoon ground ginger**
**¼ teaspoon ground allspice**
**½ cup vegetable shortening**
**½ cup chopped pecans**
**¾ cup mashed canned sweet potatoes**
**½ cup milk**

**1.** Preheat oven to 450°F.

**2.** Combine flour, sugar, baking powder, salt, cinnamon, ginger and allspice in medium bowl. Cut in shortening with pastry blender or 2 knives until mixture resembles coarse crumbs. Stir in pecans.

**3.** Combine sweet potatoes and milk in medium bowl with wire whisk until smooth.

**4.** Make well in center of flour mixture. Add sweet potato mixture; stir until soft dough forms.

**5.** Turn out dough onto well-floured surface. Knead dough gently 10 to 12 times.

**6.** Roll or pat dough to ½-inch thickness. Cut dough into rounds with lightly floured 2½-inch biscuit cutter.

**7.** Place biscuits 2 inches apart on *ungreased* large baking sheet. Bake 12 to 14 minutes or until golden brown and wooden pick inserted in center comes out clean. Remove from baking sheet. Cool on wire rack 10 minutes. Serve warm or cool completely.        *Makes about 12 biscuits*

## DILLED POPOVERS

**1 cup skim milk**
**¾ cup EGG BEATERS® Real Egg Product**
**3 tablespoons FLEISCHMANN'S® Margarine, melted**
**¾ cup all-purpose flour**
**¼ cup CREAM OF RICE® Hot Cereal**
**1 teaspoon dried dill weed**
**½ teaspoon onion powder**

In medium bowl, beat milk, Egg Beaters® and margarine until blended.

In small bowl, combine flour, cereal, dill and onion powder; beat into egg mixture until well blended. Pour into 8 well-greased 6-ounce custard cups.

Bake at 450°F for 15 minutes; *reduce heat to 350°F.* Bake for 5 to 10 minutes or until puffed and lightly browned. Carefully slit tops of popovers; bake 5 minutes more. Serve immediately.

*Makes 8 popovers*

*Sweet Potato Biscuits*

# RYE BREAD

- **2 packages active dry yeast**
- **1 tablespoon sugar**
- **1¾ cups warm water (105° to 115°F)**
- **3 cups rye flour, divided**
- **2 to 3 cups bread flour, divided**
- **½ cup molasses**
- **2 tablespoons caraway seeds**
- **2 tablespoons white vinegar**
- **2 tablespoons vegetable oil**
- **2 teaspoons salt**
- **1 egg**
- **1 egg white**
- **1 tablespoon water**
- **Additional caraway seeds (optional)**

To proof yeast, sprinkle yeast and sugar over 1¾ cups warm water in large bowl; stir until yeast is dissolved. Let stand 5 minutes or until mixture is bubbly. Gradually add 2 cups rye flour and 1 cup bread flour to yeast mixture with electric mixer at low speed. Add molasses, caraway seeds, vinegar, oil and salt; beat 1 minute. Increase speed to medium; beat 2 minutes. Reduce speed to low. Beat in 1 egg and remaining 1 cup rye flour. Increase speed to medium; beat 2 minutes. Stir in enough additional bread flour, about 1 cup, with wooden spoon to make soft dough.

Turn out dough onto lightly floured surface; flatten slightly. Knead dough 10 to 15 minutes or until smooth and elastic, adding 1 cup bread flour to prevent sticking if necessary. Shape dough into a ball. Place in large greased bowl. Turn dough over so that top is greased. Cover with towel; let rise in warm place about 1¼ hours or until doubled in bulk.

Punch down dough. Knead dough on lightly floured surface 1 minute. Cut dough in half. Cover with towel; let rest 10 minutes.

Grease large baking sheet. Shape each half into oval loaf about 9 inches long. Place loaves 6 inches apart on prepared baking sheet. Cover with towel; let rise in warm place about 1 hour or until doubled in bulk.

Preheat oven to 350°F. Combine egg white and water in small cup. Make 3 (½-inch-deep) diagonal slashes with tip of sharp knife across top of each loaf. Brush loaves with egg white mixture. Sprinkle with additional caraway seeds, if desired. Bake 30 to 35 minutes or until loaves are browned and sound hollow when tapped. Immediately remove from baking sheet; cool completely on wire racks.

*Makes 2 loaves*

*Rye Bread*

TEAM-UPS

## SCONES

    2 cups all-purpose flour
    1 tablespoon baking powder
    1 tablespoon sugar
    ½ teaspoon salt
    ¼ BUTTER FLAVOR* CRISCO® Stick or
        ¼ cup BUTTER FLAVOR CRISCO
        all-vegetable shortening
    2 eggs (1 whole, 1 separated)
    ½ cup heavy cream**

*Butter Flavor Crisco is artificially flavored.
**Use milk in place of cream for lighter scones.

1. **Heat** oven to 400°F.

2. **Combine** flour, baking powder, sugar and salt in large bowl. **Cut** in shortening with pastry blender (or two knives).

3. **Combine** whole egg, egg yolk and cream in medium bowl. **Beat** until well blended. **Add** to flour mixture. **Stir** until flour is moistened. **Work** with hands to form a ball. *Do not overwork.*

4. **Roll** dough to ½-inch thickness on lightly floured surface. **Cut** out rounds using 2-inch cutter. **Place** on *ungreased* baking sheet.

5. **Beat** egg white lightly. Brush on top of scones. Sprinkle with sugar.

6. **Bake** at 400°F. for 9 to 11 minutes or until lightly browned.                    *Makes 20 scones*

**RAISIN SCONES:** Add 2 *additional* teaspoons sugar, ¾ cup golden raisins and ¼ cup diced candied orange peel to flour mixture.

**CHEESE AND NUT SCONES:** *Decrease* sugar to 2 teaspoons. Add ½ cup crumbled blue or grated Parmesan cheese and ½ cup chopped walnuts or pecans to flour mixture.

**HERB AND CHEDDAR SCONES:** *Decrease* sugar to 2 teaspoons. Add ¾ cup shredded sharp Cheddar cheese and ¼ cup chopped fresh herbs, such as dill *or* 1 teaspoon dried herbs to flour mixture.

## PESTO SURPRISE MUFFINS

    2 cups all-purpose flour
    2 tablespoons grated Parmesan cheese
    1 tablespoon baking powder
    ½ teaspoon salt
    1 cup milk
    ¼ cup vegetable oil
    1 egg
    ¼ cup prepared pesto sauce
        Additional grated Parmesan cheese
        (optional)

Preheat oven to 400°F. Grease 12 (2½-inch) muffin cups; set aside.

Combine flour, 2 tablespoons Parmesan cheese, baking powder and salt in large bowl. Combine milk, oil and egg in small bowl until blended. Stir

TEAM-UPS

into flour mixture just until moistened. Spoon into prepared muffin cups, filling one-third full. Stir pesto sauce to blend; spoon 1 teaspoon pesto sauce into each muffin cup. Spoon remaining batter evenly over pesto sauce. Sprinkle additional Parmesan cheese over tops of muffins, if desired.

Bake 25 to 30 minutes or until golden brown and wooden pick inserted in center comes out clean. Remove from pan. Cool on wire rack 10 minutes. Serve warm or cool completely.   *Makes 12 muffins*

## PARMESAN GARLIC TWISTS

    1 cup all-purpose flour
    ½ teaspoon baking powder
    ½ teaspoon salt
    ½ teaspoon Italian seasoning*
    ¾ cup grated Parmesan cheese, divided
    ⅓ BUTTER FLAVOR** CRISCO® Stick or
        ⅓ cup BUTTER FLAVOR CRISCO
        all-vegetable shortening
    3 egg yolks
    4 garlic cloves, minced or crushed *or*
        ½ teaspoon garlic powder
    2 teaspoons water
    1 egg white
        Paprika

*Or, substitute ½ teaspoon of oregano, basil, rosemary or marjoram or some combination of these dried herbs.
**Butter Flavor Crisco in artificially flavored.

1. **Heat** oven to 400°F. **Grease** baking sheets with shortening.

2. **Combine** flour, baking powder, salt and Italian seasoning in large bowl. **Reserve** 1 tablespoon Parmesan cheese. **Add** remaining cheese. **Cut** in shortening with pastry blender (or two knives) until mixture resembles coarse crumbs. **Beat** egg yolks, garlic and water lightly. **Sprinkle** over flour mixture. **Toss** lightly with fork until dough forms a ball. **Flour** lightly.

3. **Roll** dough out on floured surface or between two sheets of waxed paper to form a 13×9-inch rectangle. **Trim** edges to straighten.

4. **Cut** in half crosswise. **Cut** strips ¼ inch wide (they will be 6½ inches long). **Twist** two strips together, overlapping each strip over the other. **Place** 2 inches apart on prepared baking sheets. **Repeat** until all strips are twists. **Brush** with egg white. **Sprinkle** with reserved Parmesan cheese.

5. **Bake** at 400°F. for 8 to 10 minutes or until lightly browned. **Cool** 1 minute before removing to cooling rack. **Cool** completely. **Sprinkle** with paprika.   *Makes 3 dozen twists*

## HERB–CHEESE BISCUIT LOAF

**1½ cups all-purpose flour**
**¼ cup grated Parmesan cheese**
**2 tablespoons yellow cornmeal**
**2 teaspoons baking powder**
**½ teaspoon salt**
**¼ cup butter or margarine**
**2 eggs**
**½ cup heavy cream**
**¾ teaspoon dried basil leaves, crushed**
**¾ teaspoon dried oregano leaves, crushed**
**⅛ teaspoon garlic powder**
**Additional Parmesan cheese (optional)**

Preheat oven to 425°F. Grease large baking sheet; set aside.

Combine flour, ¼ cup cheese, cornmeal, baking powder and salt in large bowl. Cut in butter with pastry blender or 2 knives until mixture resembles coarse crumbs. Beat eggs in medium bowl. Add cream, basil, oregano and garlic powder; beat until well blended. Add cream mixture to flour mixture; stir until mixture forms soft dough that clings together and forms a ball. Turn out dough onto well-floured surface. Knead dough gently 10 to 12 times. Place dough on prepared baking sheet. Roll or pat dough into 7-inch round, about 1 inch thick. Starting from center, score top of dough into 8 wedges with tip of sharp knife, taking care not to cut completely through dough. Sprinkle with additional cheese, if desired.

Bake 20 to 25 minutes or until toothpick inserted in center comes out clean. Cool on baking sheet on wire rack 10 minutes. Serve warm.

*Makes 8 servings*

## FETA–DILL MUFFINS

**2 cups all-purpose flour**
**2 tablespoons sugar**
**1 tablespoon baking powder**
**1 cup milk**
**½ cup (4 ounces) crumbled feta cheese**
**⅓ cup vegetable oil**
**1 tablespoon chopped fresh dill** *or*
**1 teaspoon dried dill weed**
**1 egg**

Preheat oven to 400°F. Grease or paper-line 12 (2½-inch) muffin cups; set aside.

Combine flour, sugar and baking powder in large bowl. Combine milk, cheese, oil, dill and egg in small bowl until blended. Stir into flour mixture just until moistened. Spoon evenly into prepared muffin cups.

Bake 25 to 30 minutes or until golden brown and wooden pick inserted in center comes out clean. Remove from pan. Cool on wire rack 10 minutes. Serve warm or cool completely.

*Makes 12 muffins*

*Herb-Cheese Biscuit Loaf*

TEAM-UPS

# FRENCH BREAD

**2 packages active dry yeast**
**1 tablespoon sugar**
**2½ cups warm water (105° to 115°F), divided**
**6¾ to 7½ cups bread or all-purpose flour, divided**
**2 teaspoons salt**
**2 tablespoons yellow cornmeal**
**Water**

To proof yeast, sprinkle yeast and sugar over ½ cup warm water in large bowl; stir until yeast is dissolved. Let stand 5 minutes or until mixture is bubbly. Add 2 cups flour, remaining 2 cups warm water and salt. Beat with electric mixer at low speed until blended. Increase speed to medium; beat 2 minutes.

Stir in enough additional flour, about 4¾ cups, to make soft dough. Turn out dough onto lightly floured surface; flatten slightly. Knead dough about 10 minutes or until smooth and elastic, adding ¾ cup more flour to prevent sticking if necessary. Shape dough into a ball; place in large greased bowl. Turn dough over so that top is greased. Cover with towel; let rise in warm place 1 to 1½ hours or until doubled in bulk.

Punch down dough. Knead dough in bowl 1 minute. Cover with towel; let rise in warm place about 1 hour or until doubled in bulk.

Grease two (2-loaf) French bread pans or 2 large baking sheets. Sprinkle with corn meal; set aside. Punch down dough. Turn dough onto lightly floured surface. Knead dough several times to remove air bubbles. Divide dough into 4 pieces. Cover with towel; let rest 10 minutes. Roll each piece of dough back and forth, forming loaf about 14 inches long and 2 inches in diameter. Place loaves in prepared pans or 4 inches apart on prepared baking sheets. Cut 3 (¼-inch-deep) slashes into each loaf with tip of sharp knife. Brush loaves with water. Cover with towel; let rise in warm place about 35 minutes or until doubled in bulk.

Place small baking pan on bottom of oven. Preheat oven to 450°F. Place 2 ice cubes in pan in bottom of oven. Brush loaves with water; bake 10 minutes. Rotate bread pans top to bottom. Quickly spray loaves with cool water using spray mister. Reduce oven temperature to 400°F; bake 10 minutes. Rotate bread pans again. Spray loaves with water; bake 10 to 15 minutes more or until loaves are golden brown and sound hollow when tapped. Immediately remove from bread pans; cool completely on wire racks. Serve warm.

*Makes 4 loaves*

*French Bread*

**TEAM-UPS**

# ANADAMA BREAD

**7¾ to 8¼ cups all-purpose flour, divided**
**2 packages active dry yeast**
**1½ teaspoons salt**
**2¾ cups water**
**¾ cup molasses**
**¼ cup butter or margarine**
**1¼ cups yellow cornmeal**

Combine 4 cups flour, yeast and salt in large bowl; set aside. Combine water, molasses and butter in 2-quart saucepan. Heat over low heat until mixture is 120° to 130°F. (Butter does not need to completely melt.) Gradually beat water mixture into flour mixture with electric mixer at low speed. Increase speed to medium; beat 2 minutes. Beat in cornmeal and 2 cups flour at low speed. Increase speed to medium; beat 2 minutes. Stir in enough additional flour, about 1¾ cups, with wooden spoon to make soft dough. Turn out dough onto floured surface; flatten slightly. Knead dough 8 to 10 minutes or until smooth and elastic, adding ½ cup flour to prevent sticking if necessary. Shape dough into a ball; place in large greased bowl. Turn dough over so that top is greased. Cover with towel; let rise in warm place about 1 hour or until doubled in bulk.

Punch down dough. Knead dough on well-floured surface 1 minute. Cut dough in half. Cover with towel; let rest 10 minutes.

Meanwhile, grease 2 (1½-quart) soufflé or casserole dishes; set aside. Shape each half of dough into a ball; place in prepared pans. Cover loaves with towel. Let rise in warm place about 40 minutes or until doubled in bulk.

Preheat oven to 375°F. Bake 35 to 40 minutes or until loaves are browned and sound hollow when tapped. Immediately remove from pans; cool on wire racks. *Makes 2 loaves*

# WILD RICE CHEESY BISCUITS

**2¼ cups buttermilk baking mix**
**¾ cup milk**
**1 cup shredded Cheddar cheese**
**⅔ cup well-cooked wild rice, chopped**

Preheat oven to 425°F. Grease baking sheet; set aside.

Combine baking mix, milk and cheese in large bowl until soft dough forms. Stir in wild rice. Drop tablespoonfuls of dough onto prepared baking sheet.

Bake 8 to 10 minutes or until golden brown and wooden pick inserted in center comes out clean. Remove from baking sheet. Cool on wire rack 10 minutes. Serve warm or cool completely.

*Makes 10 to 12 biscuits*

*Favorite recipe from* **Minnesota Cultivated Wild Rice Council**

*Anadama Bread*

# HONEY–MUSTARD SCONES

3½ to 3¾ cups all-purpose flour, divided
5 teaspoons DAVIS® Baking Powder
1 teaspoon salt
¾ cup margarine
3 eggs, divided
½ cup milk
⅓ cup GREY POUPON® Country Dijon Mustard
¼ cup honey
½ teaspoon A.1.® Steak Sauce
¾ cup finely chopped ham

In large bowl, mix 3½ cups flour, baking powder and salt. With pastry blender, cut in margarine until mixture resembles coarse crumbs; set aside.

In small bowl, with wire whisk, beat 2 eggs, milk, mustard, honey and steak sauce; add ham. Stir into flour mixture just until blended, adding extra flour if necessary to make soft dough.

On lightly floured surface, roll dough into 12×8-inch rectangle. Cut dough into eight 4×3-inch rectangles; cut each rectangle into 2 triangles. Place on greased baking sheets, about 2 inches apart. Beat remaining egg; brush tops of scones with egg.

Bake at 425°F for 10 minutes or until golden brown.                              *Makes 16 scones*

# ANJOU PEAR CHEESE MUFFINS

2 cups all-purpose flour
¼ cup packed brown sugar
3 teaspoons baking powder
½ teaspoon salt
¾ cup (3 ounces) shredded Swiss cheese
⅔ cup milk
1 egg, slightly beaten
2 tablespoons vegetable oil
1 USA Anjou pear, finely chopped
½ cup chopped nuts

Preheat oven to 400°F. Grease 12 (2½-inch) muffin cups; set aside.

Combine flour, sugar, baking powder, salt and cheese in large bowl. Combine milk, egg and oil in small bowl. Stir into flour mixture with pear and nuts just until moistened. Spoon evenly into prepared muffin cups.

Bake 20 to 25 minutes or until wooden pick inserted near center comes out clean. Remove from pan. Cool on wire rack 10 minutes. Serve warm or cool completely.                       *Makes 12 muffins*

**NOTE:** Anjou Pear Cheese Muffins may be frozen in aluminum foil or plastic food storage bags. Reheat, unthawed, at 350°F 20 to 25 minutes or until thoroughly heated.

*Favorite recipe from* **Oregon-Washington-California Pear Bureau**

*Honey–Mustard Scones*

TEAM-UPS

# MARBLE SWIRL BREAD

**2¾ to 3¼ cups all-purpose flour, divided**
**¼ cup sugar**
**1 package active dry yeast**
**1 teaspoon salt**
**1⅓ cups plus 1 tablespoon water, divided**
**¼ cup butter or margarine**
**1 whole egg**
**2 tablespoons molasses**
**2 teaspoons unsweetened cocoa powder**
**1 teaspoon instant coffee powder**
**1 to 1¼ cups rye flour**
**1 egg yolk**

Combine 1½ cups all-purpose flour, sugar, yeast and salt in large bowl; set aside. Combine 1⅓ cups water and butter in 1-quart saucepan. Heat over low heat until mixture is 120° to 130°F. (Butter does not need to completely melt.) Gradually beat water mixture into flour mixture with electric mixer at low speed. Increase speed to medium; beat 2 minutes. Reduce speed to low; beat in 1 egg and ½ cup all-purpose flour. Increase speed to medium; beat 2 minutes.

Reserve half of batter (about 1⅓ cups) in another bowl. Stir ¾ cup all-purpose flour into remaining batter to make stiff dough, adding remaining ½ cup all-purpose flour if necessary; set aside. To make darker dough, stir molasses, cocoa, coffee and enough rye flour, about 1¼ cups, into reserved

batter to make stiff dough. Cover doughs with towels. Let rise in warm place about 1 hour or until doubled in bulk.

Punch down doughs. Knead doughs on lightly floured surface 1 minute. Cover with towel; let rest 10 minutes. Grease large baking sheet.

Roll out lighter dough to 12×9-inch rectangle with lightly floured rolling pin; set aside. Roll darker dough into 12×8-inch rectangle; place on top of lighter dough. Starting with 1 (12-inch) side, roll up doughs together jelly-roll fashion. Pinch seam and ends to seal. Place loaf, seam side down, on prepared baking sheet, tucking ends under. Cover with towel; let rise in warm place about 45 minutes or until doubled in bulk.

Preheat oven to 350°F. For egg wash, add remaining 1 tablespoon water to egg yolk; beat until just combined. Make 3 (½-inch-deep) slashes across top of loaf with tip of sharp knife. Brush with egg yolk mixture.

Bake 35 to 40 minutes or until loaf is browned and sounds hollow when tapped. Immediately remove from baking sheet; cool completely on wire rack.

*Makes 1 loaf*

*Marble Swirl Bread*

## TEAM-UPS

## DINNER ROLLS

**3¾ to 4¼ cups all-purpose flour, divided**
**¼ cup sugar**
**2 packages active dry yeast**
**1 teaspoon salt**
**1¼ cups milk**
**½ cup vegetable shortening**
**2 eggs**

Combine 1½ cups flour, sugar, yeast and salt in large bowl; set aside. Combine milk and shortening in 1-quart saucepan. Heat over low heat until mixture is 120° to 130°F. (Shortening does not need to completely melt.) Gradually beat milk mixture into flour mixture with electric mixer at low speed. Increase speed to medium; beat well. Reduce speed to low. Beat in eggs and 1 cup flour. Increase speed to medium; beat 2 minutes.

Stir in enough additional all-purpose flour, about 1¼ cups, with wooden spoon to make soft dough. Turn out dough onto lightly floured surface; flatten slightly. Knead dough about 5 minutes or until smooth and elastic, adding ½ cup more all-purpose flour to prevent sticking if necessary. Shape dough into a ball. Place in large greased bowl. Turn dough over so that top is greased. Cover with towel. Let rise in warm place about 1 hour or until doubled in bulk.

Punch down dough. Knead dough on lightly floured surface 1 minute. Cut dough in half. Cover with towel; let rest 10 minutes.

Shape rolls as desired: see Crescents, Cloverleaf and Fan-Tans. Cover rolls with towel; let rise in warm place about 30 minutes or until doubled in bulk.

Preheat oven to 375°F. Bake on 2 racks in oven 15 to 20 minutes or until rolls are golden brown and sound hollow when tapped. (Rotate baking sheets halfway through baking.) Immediately remove from pans or baking sheets; cool on wire racks 10 minutes. Serve warm.

**CRESCENTS:** Grease 2 large baking sheets. Melt 2 tablespoons butter or margarine; set aside. Cut dough in half. Roll out half of dough into 16-inch circle with lightly floured rolling pin; keep remaining half covered with towel. Brush circle with 1 tablespoon melted butter; cut into 12 wedges. Roll up each wedge, starting at wide end and rolling toward point. Place rolled wedges, point end down, about 2 inches apart on prepared baking sheets; curve ends to form crescents. Repeat with remaining dough and butter. Makes 24 rolls.

**CLOVERLEAF:** Grease 24 (2½-inch) muffin pan cups. Cut dough in half. Cut half of dough into 36 pieces, keeping remaining half covered with towel. Shape each piece into a ball, pulling down edges and tucking them under to make tops smooth. Arrange 3 balls in each prepared muffin cup. Repeat with remaining dough. Makes 24 rolls.

**FAN-TANS:** Grease 24 (2½-inch) muffin pan cups. Melt 2 tablespoons butter or margarine; set aside. Cut dough in half. Roll out half of dough into 15×12-inch rectangle on lightly floured surface with lightly floured rolling pin, keeping remaining half covered with towel. Brush with 1 tablespoon melted butter. Cut rectangle lengthwise into 5 strips; stack strips evenly on top of each other, buttered side up. Cut stack into 12 squares. Place squares, cut side up, in prepared muffin pans. Repeat with remaining dough and butter. Makes 24 rolls.

## TABASCO® CORN BREAD WEDGES

- **1 package corn bread mix**
- **1 cup (4 ounces) finely shredded sharp Cheddar cheese**
- **¼ cup butter or margarine**
- **¼ teaspoon Worcestershire sauce**
- **¼ teaspoon TABASCO® pepper sauce**
- **1 egg white, stiffly beaten**
- **Paprika**

Prepare corn bread according to package directions; bake in 9-inch pie plate. Remove corn bread when done. Cool in pan on wire rack 10 minutes. Cut into 8 wedges.

Meanwhile, combine cheese, butter, Worcestershire sauce and Tabasco® sauce in small bowl, beating until smooth. Fold in egg white. Spread cheese mixture evenly over wedges. Sprinkle with paprika.

Preheat broiler to 400°F; broil corn bread about 4 minutes or until cheese topping is puffy and golden brown. Serve warm. *Makes 8 wedges*

## SAVORY PUMPKIN BACON MUFFINS

- **1¾ cups all-purpose flour**
- **¼ cup sugar**
- **2 teaspoons baking powder**
- **¾ teaspoon ground nutmeg**
- **½ teaspoon salt**
- **⅔ cup solid pack pumpkin**
- **⅔ cup milk**
- **¼ cup vegetable oil**
- **1 egg, beaten**
- **½ cup cooked crumbled bacon**

Preheat oven to 425°F. Grease or paper-line 24 (1¾-inch) mini-muffin cups; set aside.

Combine flour, sugar, baking powder, nutmeg and salt in large bowl. Combine pumpkin, milk, oil and egg in small bowl until blended. Stir into flour mixture just until moistened. Fold in bacon. Spoon into prepared muffin cups, filling almost full.

Bake 16 to 18 minutes or until wooden pick inserted in center comes out clean. Remove from pans. Cool on wire racks 10 minutes. Serve warm or cool completely. *Makes 24 mini-muffins*

TEAM-UPS

## CHEDDAR CHEESE PEPPER BREAD

½ **cup (1 stick) butter**
2½ **cups all-purpose flour**
2½ **teaspoons baking powder**
 1 to 1½ **teaspoons ground black pepper**
 ¾ **teaspoon baking soda**
 ¾ **teaspoon salt**
 2 **cups (about 8 ounces) shredded sharp Cheddar cheese**
 2 **eggs**
 1 **container (8 ounces) plain yogurt**

Preheat oven to 375°F. Butter and flour 9×5×3-inch loaf pan; set aside. Melt butter in small saucepan over low heat; set aside to cool. Combine flour, baking powder, black pepper, baking soda and salt in large bowl; stir in Cheddar cheese. In medium bowl, lightly beat eggs; stir in yogurt and melted butter. Stir into flour mixture just until moistened. Spoon into prepared pan.

Bake 35 minutes or until golden brown and wooden pick inserted in center comes out clean. Cool in pan on wire rack 10 minutes; remove from pan. Serve warm or toasted, if desired.

*Makes 1 loaf (16 slices)*

**ROLLED BISCUITS:** Butter large baking sheet; set aside. Prepare dough as directed. Place dough on lightly floured surface; roll or pat dough to ½-inch thickness. Cut out rounds with lightly floured 2½-inch biscuit cutter; place 1 inch apart onto prepared baking sheet. Bake 15 to 18 minutes. Continue as directed. *Makes 16 biscuits*

**DROP BISCUITS:** Butter large baking sheet; set aside. Drop ¼-cupfuls of dough 1 inch apart onto prepared baking sheet. Bake 15 to 18 minutes. Continue as directed. *Makes 16 biscuits*

**SWISS CARAWAY BREAD OR BISCUITS:** Substitute Swiss cheese for Cheddar cheese; omit black pepper. Add 1½ teaspoons caraway seeds to flour mixture. Add 1 tablespoon prepared Dijon mustard to yogurt mixture. Bake as bread or biscuits as directed. *Makes 1 loaf or 16 biscuits*

*Favorite recipe from* **National Dairy Board**

*Cheddar Cheese Pepper Bread*

TEAM-UPS

## CARAWAY CHEESE MUFFINS

1¼ cups all-purpose flour
½ cup rye flour
2 tablespoons sugar
2½ teaspoons baking powder
½ teaspoon salt
1 cup (4 ounces) shredded sharp Cheddar
    or Swiss cheese
1½ teaspoons caraway seeds
1 cup milk
¼ cup vegetable oil
1 egg

Preheat oven to 400°F. Grease or paper-line 12 (2½-inch) muffin cups; set aside.

Combine flours, sugar, baking powder and salt in large bowl. Add cheese and caraway seeds; toss to coat. Combine milk, oil and egg in small bowl until well blended. Stir into flour mixture just until moistened. Spoon evenly into prepared muffin cups.

Bake 20 to 25 minutes or until golden brown and wooden pick inserted in center comes out clean. Remove from pan. Cool on wire rack 10 minutes. Serve warm or cool completely.

*Makes 12 muffins*

## SQUASH MUFFINS

1 cup all-purpose flour
1 cup whole wheat flour
⅓ cup packed brown sugar
2 teaspoons baking powder
1½ teaspoons ground cinnamon
½ teaspoon baking soda
½ teaspoon salt
½ teaspoon ground cloves
¼ teaspoon ground nutmeg
6 tablespoons butter or margarine
½ cup golden raisins
¾ cup milk
½ of 12-ounce package frozen cooked
    squash, thawed and well drained
    (½ cup)
1 egg

Preheat oven to 400°F. Grease or paper-line 12 (2½-inch) muffin cups; set aside.

Combine flours, sugar, baking powder, cinnamon, baking soda, salt, cloves and nutmeg in large bowl. Cut in butter with pastry blender or 2 knives until mixture resembles fine crumbs. Stir in raisins. Combine milk, squash and egg in small bowl until blended. Stir into flour mixture just until moistened. Spoon evenly into prepared muffin cups.

Bake 25 to 30 minutes or until golden brown and wooden pick inserted in center comes out clean. Remove from pan. Cool on wire rack 10 minutes. Serve warm or cool completely. *Makes 12 muffins*

*Caraway Cheese Muffins*

TEAM-UPS

## DILL SOUR CREAM SCONES

 2 cups all-purpose flour
 2 teaspoons baking powder
 ½ teaspoon baking soda
 ½ teaspoon salt
 4 tablespoons butter or margarine
 2 eggs
 ½ cup sour cream
 1 tablespoon chopped fresh dill *or*
  1 teaspoon dried dill weed

Preheat oven to 425°F. Combine flour, baking powder, baking soda and salt. Cut in butter with pastry blender or 2 knives until mixture resembles coarse crumbs. Beat eggs with fork in small bowl. Add sour cream and dill; beat until well combined. Stir into flour mixture until mixture forms soft dough that pulls away from side of bowl.

Turn out dough onto well-floured surface. Knead dough 10 times.* Roll out dough into 9×6-inch rectangle with lightly floured rolling pin. Cut dough into 6 (3-inch) squares. Cut each square diagonally in half, making 12 triangles. Place triangles 2 inches apart onto *ungreased* baking sheets.

Bake 10 to 12 minutes or until golden brown and wooden pick inserted in center comes out clean. Remove from baking sheets. Cool on wire rack 10 minutes. Serve warm or cool completely.

*Makes 12 scones*

*To knead dough, fold dough in half toward you and press dough away from you with heels of hands. Give dough a quarter turn and continue folding, pressing and turning.

## ZUCCHINI CHEESE MUFFINS

 1 cup all-purpose flour
 ¾ cup PROGRESSO® Italian Style or Plain
  Bread Crumbs
 ¾ cup sugar
 1½ teaspoons baking powder
 1 teaspoon salt
 1 cup (4 ounces) shredded Cheddar cheese
 2 eggs, beaten
 1 can (5 fluid ounces) PET® Evaporated Milk
 ¼ cup butter, melted
 1½ cups shredded zucchini

Preheat oven to 400°F. Grease 18 (2½-inch) muffin cups.

Combine flour, bread crumbs, sugar, baking powder and salt in large bowl; stir in cheese. Combine eggs, evaporated milk and butter in medium bowl; stir in zucchini. Add zucchini mixture to flour mixture; stir until moistened. Spoon evenly into prepared muffin cups.

Bake 20 to 22 minutes or until lightly browned. Remove from pan. Serve warm.

*Makes 18 muffins*

*Dill Sour Cream Scones*

TEAM-UPS

## ROASTED GARLIC BREAD STICKS

    1 large head garlic (about 14 to 16 cloves)
    3 tablespoons olive oil, divided
    3 tablespoons water, divided
    1 tablespoon butter or margarine, softened
    1 package active dry yeast
    1 teaspoon sugar
    1 cup warm water (105° to 115°F)
2½ to 3 cups all-purpose flour, divided
    1 teaspoon salt
    1 egg white
    1 tablespoon sesame seeds

Preheat oven to 350°F. Remove outer papery skin from garlic head. Place garlic in 10-ounce ovenproof custard cup. Drizzle garlic with 1 tablespoon olive oil and 2 tablespoons water. Cover tightly with foil. Bake 1 hour or until garlic cloves are tender. Remove foil and let cool.

When garlic is cool enough to handle, break into cloves. Squeeze skin of each clove until garlic pops out. Finely chop garlic cloves. (Makes about ⅓ cup.) Combine chopped garlic and butter in small bowl. Cover; set aside.

To proof yeast, sprinkle yeast and sugar over 1 cup warm water in large bowl; stir until yeast is dissolved. Let stand 5 minutes or until mixture is bubbly. Beat in 1½ cups flour, salt and remaining 2 tablespoons olive oil with electric mixer at low speed until blended, scraping down side of bowl once. Increase speed to medium; beat 2 minutes.

Stir in enough additional flour, about 1 cup, to make soft dough.

Turn out dough onto lightly floured surface; flatten slightly. Knead dough about 5 minutes or until smooth and elastic, adding ½ cup more flour to prevent sticking if necessary. Shape dough into a ball; place in large greased bowl. Turn dough over so that top is greased. Cover with towel; let rise in warm place about 1 hour or until doubled in bulk.

Punch down dough. Knead dough on lightly floured surface 1 minute. Cover with towel; let rest 10 minutes. Grease large baking sheet; set aside.

Roll dough into 12-inch square with lightly floured rolling pin. Spread garlic mixture evenly over dough with small metal spatula or butter knife. Fold square in half. Roll dough into 14×7-inch rectangle. Cut dough crosswise into 7×1-inch strips with pizza cutter or sharp knife. Holding ends of each strip, twist 3 to 4 times. Place strips 2 inches apart on prepared baking sheet, pressing both ends to seal. Cover with towel; let rise in warm place about 30 minutes or until doubled in bulk.

Preheat oven to 400°F. Combine egg white and remaining 1 tablespoon water in small bowl. Brush sticks with egg white mixture; sprinkle with sesame seeds.

Bake 20 to 22 minutes or until golden. Serve immediately.                    *Makes 14 bread sticks*

*Roasted Garlic Bread Sticks*

# TOMATO–CARROT MUFFIN TOPS

**1 large (about 8 ounces) fresh Florida tomato, ripened at room temperature until bright red**
**⅓ cup low fat milk**
**1 egg**
**2 tablespoons vegetable oil**
**2 cups buttermilk baking mix**
**½ cup packed brown sugar**
**1 teaspoon ground cinnamon**
**¼ cup shredded carrot**

**1.** Preheat oven to 400°F. Spray 2 large baking sheets with nonstick cooking spray; set aside.

**2.** Core tomato; chop. Measure 1¼ cups tomato; set aside.

**3.** In small bowl combine milk, egg and oil until well blended; set aside.

**4.** In large bowl combine baking mix, sugar and cinnamon. Stir into milk mixture just until moistened. Stir in carrot and reserved tomato.

**5.** Drop ¼-cupfuls of batter 1 inch apart onto prepared baking sheets. Bake 10 minutes or until golden brown and wooden pick inserted in center comes out clean. Cool on baking sheets 1 minute; remove. Cool on wire racks 10 minutes. Serve warm or cool completely.    *Makes 12 muffin tops*

*Favorite recipe from **Florida Tomato Committee***

# APPLE CHEDDAR SCONES

**1½ cups unsifted all-purpose flour**
**½ cup toasted wheat germ**
**3 tablespoons sugar**
**2 teaspoons baking powder**
**½ teaspoon salt**
**2 tablespoons butter**
**1 small Rome Beauty apple, cored and chopped**
**¼ cup shredded Cheddar cheese**
**1 large egg white**
**½ cup low fat (1%) milk**

**1.** Heat oven to 400°F. Grease 8-inch round cake pan. In medium bowl, combine flour, wheat germ, sugar, baking powder and salt. With two knives or pastry blender, cut in butter until the size of coarse crumbs. Toss chopped apple and cheese in flour mixture.

**2.** Beat together egg white and milk until well combined. Add to flour mixture, mixing with fork until dough forms. Turn dough out onto lightly floured surface and knead 6 times.

**3.** Spread dough evenly in cake pan and score deeply with knife into 6 wedges. Bake 25 to 30 minutes or until top springs back when gently pressed. Let stand 5 minutes; remove from pan and cool before serving.    *Makes 6 scones*

*Favorite recipe from **Washington Apple Commission***

*Tomato-Carrot Muffin Top*

**TEAM-UPS**

# SUN–DRIED TOMATO 'N' CHEESE MUFFINS

1 jar (7½ ounces) sun-dried tomatoes
 packed in olive oil
2 tablespoons butter or margarine
¼ teaspoon dried rosemary leaves
1 clove garlic, minced
2 cups all-purpose flour
2 tablespoons sugar
2 teaspoons baking powder
½ teaspoon baking soda
½ teaspoon salt
1 cup (4 ounces) shredded provolone
 cheese
1 cup buttermilk
1 egg

Drain tomatoes; reserve 2 tablespoons oil. Chop enough tomatoes to measure ⅓ cup; set aside.

Heat reserved oil and butter in small saucepan over medium-low heat. Cook and stir rosemary and garlic 30 seconds until garlic is soft. Remove saucepan from heat; set aside.

Preheat oven to 400°F. Grease or paper-line 12 (2½-inch) muffin cups; set aside.

Combine flour, sugar, baking powder, baking soda and salt in large bowl; stir in cheese. Combine buttermilk and egg in small bowl until blended; stir in tomatoes and garlic mixture. Stir tomato mixture into flour mixture just until moistened. Spoon evenly into prepared muffin cups.

Bake 20 to 25 minutes or until golden brown and toothpick inserted in center comes out clean. Remove from pan. Cool on wire rack 10 minutes. Serve warm or cool completely.

*Makes 12 muffins*

# APPLE & RAISIN SCONES

½ cup dried apples
1½ cups KRETSCHMER® Original or Honey
 Crunch Wheat Germ
½ cup whole wheat flour
¼ cup sugar
1 tablespoon baking powder
⅓ cup (5⅓ tablespoons) margarine
½ cup raisins
⅓ cup 2% low fat milk
2 egg whites, slightly beaten

Heat oven to 400°F. Coarsely chop apples; set aside.

Combine dry ingredients; cut in margarine until mixture resembles coarse crumbs. Stir in raisins and reserved apples. Add combined milk and egg whites, mixing just until moistened.

Turn dough out onto ungreased baking sheet; pat into 9-inch circle. Cut into eight wedges; do not separate.

Bake 12 to 15 minutes or until light golden brown. Break apart; serve warm with margarine, fruit spread or honey, if desired. *Makes 8 scones*

TEAM-UPS

## PARMESAN CHEESE SCONES

**2 cups all-purpose flour**
**¾ cup grated Parmesan cheese**
**2 teaspoons baking powder**
**1 teaspoon dried oregano leaves**
**¼ teaspoon salt**
**4 tablespoons chilled butter, cut into pieces**
**½ cup milk**
**2 large eggs, lightly beaten**
**¾ teaspoon TABASCO® pepper sauce**
**¾ cup finely chopped onion**

Preheat oven to 400°F. Grease baking sheet; set aside.

Combine flour, cheese, baking powder, oregano and salt in large bowl or food processor. Cut in butter with pastry blender, two knives or pulses of the food processor until mixture resembles coarse crumbs. (If blended in food processor, transfer mixture to large bowl.)

Combine milk, eggs and Tabasco® pepper sauce in small bowl until well blended; stir into flour mixture just until moistened. Stir in onion. (The dough will be sticky.)

Place dough onto center of prepared baking sheet; pat dough into 9-inch circle. Cut circle into 8 wedges. Bake 20 to 25 minutes or until golden brown and wooden pick inserted in center comes out clean. Remove from baking sheet. Cool on wire rack 10 minutes. Serve warm or cool completely.

*Makes 8 scones*

## SPANISH OLIVE CHEDDAR MUFFINS

**2 cups all-purpose flour**
**1 tablespoon sugar**
**2 teaspoons baking powder**
**1 teaspoon dry mustard**
**½ teaspoon baking soda**
**½ teaspoon salt**
**⅛ teaspoon ground red pepper**
**¼ cup butter or margarine, softened**
**1 cup (4 ounces) shredded sharp Cheddar cheese**
**½ cup chopped pimiento-stuffed olives**
**1 cup buttermilk**
**1 egg**

Preheat oven to 375°F. Grease or paper-line 12 (2½-inch) muffin cups; set aside.

Combine flour, sugar, baking powder, mustard, baking soda, salt and red pepper in large bowl. Cut in butter with pastry blender or 2 knives until mixture resembles fine crumbs. Stir in cheese and olives. Combine buttermilk and egg in small bowl until well blended. Stir into flour mixture just until moistened. Spoon evenly into prepared muffin cups.

Bake 25 to 30 minutes or until golden brown and wooden pick inserted in center comes out clean. Remove from pan. Cool on wire rack 10 minutes. Serve warm or cool completely.

*Makes 12 muffins*

## TEAM-UPS

## PUMPKIN–GINGER SCONES

**½ cup sugar, divided**
**2 cups all-purpose flour**
**2 teaspoons baking powder**
**1 teaspoon ground cinnamon**
**½ teaspoon baking soda**
**½ teaspoon salt**
**5 tablespoons butter or margarine, divided**
**1 egg**
**½ cup solid pack pumpkin**
**¼ cup sour cream**
**½ teaspoon grated fresh ginger** *or*
**2 tablespoons finely chopped crystallized ginger**

Preheat oven to 425°F. Reserve 1 tablespoon sugar. Combine remaining sugar, flour, baking powder, cinnamon, baking soda and salt in large bowl. Cut in 4 tablespoons butter with pastry blender or 2 knives until mixture resembles coarse crumbs. Beat egg in small bowl; add pumpkin, sour cream and ginger. Beat until well blended. Add pumpkin mixture to flour mixture; stir until soft dough forms.

Turn out dough onto well-floured surface; knead 10 times. Roll out dough into 9×6-inch rectangle with lightly floured rolling pin. Cut dough into 6 (3-inch) squares with lightly floured knife. Cut each square diagonally in half, making 12 triangles. Place triangles 2 inches apart on *ungreased* baking sheet. Melt remaining 1 tablespoon butter. Brush triangles with butter; sprinkle with reserved sugar.

Bake 10 to 12 minutes or until golden brown and wooden pick inserted in center comes out clean. Cool on wire rack 10 minutes. Serve warm or cool completely. *Makes 12 scones*

## INDIAN CORN MUFFINS

**1 cup all-purpose flour**
**1 cup cornmeal**
**⅓ cup granulated sugar**
**1 tablespoon baking powder**
**½ teaspoon salt**
**2 eggs, lightly beaten**
**1 cup LIBBY'S® Solid Pack Pumpkin**
**¼ cup vegetable oil**
**¼ cup water**

In large bowl, combine flour, cornmeal, sugar, baking powder and salt. Mix well; set aside. In small mixer bowl, combine eggs, pumpkin, oil and water; beat well. Add wet ingredients to dry ingredients; mix thoroughly. Spoon batter into 10 greased or paper-lined muffin cups.

Bake in preheated 375°F. oven for 25 to 30 minutes or until toothpick comes out clean. Serve warm. *Makes 10 muffins*

*Pumpkin-Ginger Scones*

# LIGHT DELIGHTS

## BLUEBERRY YOGURT MUFFINS

- **2 cups QUAKER® Oat Bran hot cereal, uncooked**
- **¼ cup firmly packed brown sugar**
- **2 teaspoons baking powder**
- **1 carton (8 ounces) plain low fat yogurt**
- **2 egg whites, slightly beaten**
- **¼ cup skim milk**
- **¼ cup honey**
- **2 tablespoons vegetable oil**
- **1 teaspoon grated lemon peel**
- **½ cup fresh or frozen blueberries**

Heat oven to 425°F. Line 12 medium muffin cups with paper baking cups. Combine oat bran, brown sugar and baking powder. Add combined yogurt, egg whites, skim milk, honey, oil and lemon peel, mixing just until moistened. Fold in blueberries. Fill muffin cups almost full. Bake 18 to 20 minutes or until golden brown.

*Makes 12 muffins*

| **NUTRIENTS PER MUFFIN:** | |
| --- | --- |
| Calories | 130 |
| % of Calories from Fat | 25 |
| Total Fat | 4 g |

LIGHT DELIGHTS

## WHOLE WHEAT HERB BREAD

⅔ cup water
⅔ cup skim milk
2 teaspoons sugar
2 envelopes active dry yeast
3 egg whites, lightly beaten
3 tablespoons olive oil
1 teaspoon salt
½ teaspoon dried basil
½ teaspoon dried oregano leaves
4 to 4½ cups whole wheat flour

1. Bring water to a boil in small saucepan. Remove from heat; stir in milk and sugar. When mixture is warm (110° to 115°F), add yeast. Mix well; let stand 10 minutes or until bubbly.

2. Combine egg whites, oil, salt, basil and oregano in large bowl until well blended. Add yeast mixture; mix well. Add 4 cups flour, ½ cup at a time, mixing well after each addition, until dough is no longer sticky. Knead about 5 minutes or until smooth and elastic, adding more flour if dough is sticky. Form into a ball. Cover and let rise in warm place about 1 hour or until doubled in bulk.

3. Preheat oven to 350°F. Punch dough down and place on lightly floured surface. Divide into 4 pieces and roll each piece into a ball. Place on baking sheet sprayed with nonstick cooking spray. Bake 30 to 35 minutes until golden brown.

*Makes 24 servings*

**NUTRIENTS PER SERVING:**

| | |
|---|---|
| Calories | 99 |
| % of Calories from Fat | 18 |
| Total Fat | 2 g |

## MOTT'S® BEST EVER STRAWBERRY MUFFINS

2 cups all-purpose flour
1 cup sugar
1 teaspoon baking soda
1 teaspoon ground cinnamon
½ teaspoon salt
½ teaspoon ground nutmeg
½ cup nonfat buttermilk
½ cup MOTT'S® Natural Apple Sauce
3 egg whites
½ cup strawberry jam

1. Preheat oven to 350°F. Spray 12-cup muffin pan with nonstick cooking spray or paper-line; set aside.

2. In large bowl, combine flour, sugar, baking soda, cinnamon, salt and nutmeg.

3. In medium bowl, combine buttermilk, apple sauce and egg whites until well blended.

4. Stir apple sauce mixture into flour mixture just until moistened. Fold in strawberry jam.

5. Fill prepared muffin cups ¾ full.

6. Bake 18 to 20 minutes or until golden brown and wooden pick inserted in center comes out clean. Remove from pan. Cool on wire rack 10 minutes. Serve warm or cool completely.

*Makes 12 muffins*

**NUTRIENTS PER MUFFIN:**

| | |
|---|---|
| Calories | 190 |
| % of Calories from Fat | 2 |
| Total Fat | <1 g |

*Whole Wheat Herb Bread*

# APPLE SAUCE CINNAMON ROLLS

## ROLLS

- 4 cups all-purpose flour, divided
- 1 package active dry yeast
- 1 cup MOTT'S® Natural Apple Sauce, divided
- ½ cup skim milk
- ⅓ cup plus 2 tablespoons granulated sugar, divided
- 2 tablespoons margarine
- ½ teaspoon salt
- 1 egg, beaten lightly
- 2 teaspoons ground cinnamon

## ICING

- 1 cup sifted powdered sugar
- 1 tablespoon skim milk
- ½ teaspoon vanilla extract

**1.** To prepare rolls, in large bowl, combine 1½ cups flour and yeast. In small saucepan, combine ¾ cup applesauce, ½ cup milk, 2 tablespoons granulated sugar, margarine and salt. Cook over medium heat, stirring frequently, until mixture reaches 120° to 130°F and margarine is almost melted. (Milk will appear curdled.) Add to flour mixture along with egg. Beat with electric mixer on low speed 30 seconds, scraping bowl frequently. Beat on high speed 3 minutes. Stir in 2¼ cups flour until soft dough forms.

**2.** Turn out dough onto lightly floured surface; flatten slightly. Knead 3 to 5 minutes or until smooth and elastic, adding remaining ¼ cup flour to prevent sticking if necessary. Shape dough into ball; place in large bowl sprayed with nonstick cooking spray. Turn dough over so that top is greased. Cover with towel; let rise in warm place about 1 hour or until doubled in bulk.

**3.** Punch down dough; turn out onto lightly floured surface. Cover with towel; let rise 10 minutes. Roll out dough into 12-inch square. Spread remaining ¼ cup apple sauce over dough, to within ½ inch of edges. Combine remaining ⅓ cup granulated sugar and cinnamon; sprinkle over apple sauce. Roll up dough jelly-roll style. Moisten edge with water; pinch to seal. Cut roll into 12 (1-inch) slices. Spray two 8- or 9-inch round baking pans with nonstick cooking spray. Arrange 6 rolls ½ inch apart in each prepared pan. Cover with towel; let rise in warm place about 20 minutes or until nearly doubled.

**4.** Preheat oven to 375°F. Bake 20 to 25 minutes or until lightly browned. Cool on wire rack 5 minutes. Invert each pan onto serving plate.

**5.** To prepare icing, combine powdered sugar, 1 tablespoon milk and vanilla. Drizzle over tops of rolls. Serve warm. *Makes 12 servings*

### NUTRIENTS PER ROLL:

| | |
|---|---|
| Calories | 260 |
| % of Calories from Fat | 10 |
| Total Fat | 3 g |

*Apple Sauce Cinnamon Rolls*

## LIGHT DELIGHTS

# SESAME CRUNCH BANANA MUFFINS

**Sesame Crunch Topping (recipe follows)**
**1½ cups uncooked rolled oats**
**½ cup all-purpose flour**
**½ cup whole wheat flour**
**2 tablespoons granulated sugar**
**1 tablespoon baking powder**
**½ teaspoon salt**
**2 medium, ripe bananas, mashed**
**1 cup low fat milk**
**2 egg whites**
**2 tablespoons vegetable oil**
**1 teaspoon vanilla**

Prepare Sesame Crunch Topping; set aside. Preheat oven to 400°F. Spray muffin cups with nonstick cooking spray or paper-line; set aside.

Combine oats, flours, sugar, baking powder and salt in large bowl. Combine bananas, milk, egg whites, oil and vanilla in medium bowl until well blended. Stir into oat mixture just until moistened. (Batter will be lumpy.) Spoon evenly into prepared muffin cups, filling three-fourths full. Sprinkle 2 teaspoons Sesame Crunch over top of each muffin.

Bake 20 to 25 minutes or until golden brown and wooden pick inserted in center comes out clean. Cool in pan 5 minutes; remove. Cool on wire rack 10 minutes. Serve warm or cool completely.

*Makes 17 muffins*

Sesame Crunch Topping

**4 tablespoons packed brown sugar**
**2 tablespoons chopped walnuts**
**2 tablespoons whole wheat flour**
**1 tablespoon sesame seeds**
**1 tablespoon margarine**
**¼ teaspoon ground nutmeg**
**¼ teaspoon ground cinnamon**

Combine all ingredients in small bowl until well blended. *Makes about ¾ cup*

| NUTRIENTS PER MUFFIN: | |
| --- | --- |
| Calories | 124 |
| % of Calories from Fat | 28 |
| Total Fat | 4 g |

*Sesame Crunch Banana Muffins*

# LIGHT DELIGHTS

## PEAR SCONES

1 pear, cored
2½ cups all-purpose flour
1 cup granulated sugar
½ cup whole wheat flour
1 tablespoon baking powder
½ teaspoon baking soda
½ teaspoon ground ginger
2 tablespoons cold margarine
2 tablespoons cold butter
½ cup buttermilk
1 tablespoon granulated sugar

Preheat oven to 400°F. Spray baking sheets with nonstick cooking spray; set aside. In food processor shred pear. Remove from work bowl; set aside. In food processor combine all-purpose flour, 1 cup sugar, whole wheat flour, baking powder, baking soda and ginger; process until blended. Add margarine and butter; process until mixture resembles coarse crumbs. Transfer to large bowl. Stir in reserved pear and buttermilk until soft dough forms.

Knead dough on lightly floured surface 8 to 10 times. Roll out to ½-inch thickness; cut into rounds with biscuit cutter. Sprinkle remaining 1 tablespoon sugar over tops of scones. Bake 10 to 15 minutes or until golden brown.

*Makes about 30 scones*

### NUTRIENTS PER SCONE:

| | |
|---|---|
| Calories | 89 |
| % of Calories from Fat | 17 |
| Total Fat | 2 g |

*Favorite recipe from* **The Sugar Association, Inc.**

## CARROT ZUCCHINI MUFFINS

**MUFFINS**
2 tablespoons CRISCO® all-vegetable shortening
½ cup firmly packed brown sugar
2 egg whites, lightly beaten
⅔ cup skim milk
1¾ cups QUAKER® Oats (quick or old fashioned, uncooked)
1 cup all-purpose flour
1 tablespoon baking powder
¼ teaspoon nutmeg
1 cup shredded carrot (about 1 large)
½ cup shredded zucchini (about 1 small)

**TOPPING**
¼ cup QUAKER® Oats (quick or old fashioned, uncooked)
1 tablespoon chopped almonds
1 tablespoon CRISCO® all-vegetable shortening, melted

**1. Heat** oven to 400°F. **Line** 12 medium (about 2½-inch) muffin cups with foil or paper liners.

**2. *For muffins,* combine** 2 tablespoons shortening and brown sugar in large bowl. **Beat** at medium speed of electric mixer or **stir** with fork until well blended. **Stir** in egg whites and milk gradually.

**3. Combine** 1¾ cups oats, flour, baking powder and nutmeg. **Stir** into liquid ingredients. **Add** carrot and zucchini. **Stir** until just blended. **Fill** muffin cups almost full.

**4.** *For topping,* **combine** ¼ cup oats, nuts and 1 tablespoon shortening. **Sprinkle** over each muffin. **Press** into batter lightly.

**5. Bake** at 400°F. for 20 to 25 minutes or until golden brown. Serve warm.     *Makes 12 muffins*

**NOTE:** Baked muffins can be frozen. To reheat, microwave on HIGH about 30 seconds per muffin.

| NUTRIENTS PER MUFFIN: | |
| --- | --- |
| Calories | 177 |
| % of Calories from Fat | 27 |
| Total Fat | 5 g |

## MOTT'S® LUSCIOUS LEMON LITE MUFFINS

### MUFFINS
     1 cup all-purpose flour
     1 cup uncooked rolled oats
     ⅔ cup golden raisins
     ½ cup granulated sugar
     ¼ cup wheat germ
  1½ teaspoon baking soda
     1 teaspoon baking powder
     1 cup MOTT'S® Natural Apple Sauce
     ½ cup frozen lemonade concentrate, thawed
     ⅓ cup nonfat buttermilk
     1 egg
     1 egg white, lightly beaten
     2 tablespoons vegetable oil
     ½ teaspoon lemon extract
### GLAZE
     ½ cup confectioners' sugar
     2 to 3 tablespoons frozen lemonade
          concentrate, thawed

**1.** Preheat oven to 375°F. Spray 12-cup muffin pan with nonstick cooking spray or paper-line; set aside.

**2.** In large bowl, combine flour, oats, raisins, granulated sugar, wheat germ, baking soda and baking powser.

**3.** In medium bowl, combine apple sauce, 1/2 cup lemonade concentrate, buttermilk, egg, egg white, oil and lemon extract until well blended.

**4.** Stir apple sauce mixture into flour mixture just until moistened.

**5.** Fill muffin cups ¾ full.

**6.** Bake 17 to 20 minutes or until golden brown and wooden pick inserted in center comes out clean. Remove from pan. Cool on wire rack 10 minutes. Meanwhile, combine confectioners' sugar and 2 tablspoons lemonade concentrate; drizzle over top of each muffin. Serve warm or cool completely.     *Makes 12 muffins*

| NUTRIENTS PER MUFFIN: | |
| --- | --- |
| Calories | 230 |
| % of Calories from Fat | 16 |
| Total Fat | 4 g |

*LIGHT DELIGHTS*

## OATMEAL APPLE CRANBERRY SCONES

**2 cups all-purpose flour**
**1 cup uncooked rolled oats**
**⅓ cup sugar**
**2 teaspoons baking powder**
**½ teaspoon salt**
**½ teaspoon baking soda**
**½ teaspoon ground cinnamon**
**¾ cup MOTT'S® Natural Apple Sauce, divided**
**2 tablespoons margarine**
**½ cup coarsely chopped cranberries**
**½ cup peeled, chopped apple**
**¼ cup skim milk**
**¼ cup plus 2 tablespoons honey, divided**

**1.** Preheat oven to 425°F. Spray baking sheet with nonstick cooking spray.

**2.** In large bowl, combine flour, oats, sugar, baking powder, salt, baking soda and cinnamon. Add ½ cup apple sauce and margarine; cut in with pastry blender or fork until mixture resembles coarse crumbs. Stir in cranberries and apple.

**3.** In small bowl, combine milk and ¼ cup honey. Add milk mixture to flour mixture; stir together until dough forms a ball.

**4.** Turn out dough onto well-floured surface; knead 10 to 12 times. Pat dough into 8-inch circle. Place on prepared baking sheet. Use tip of knife to score dough into 12 wedges.

**5.** In another small bowl, combine remaining ¼ cup apple sauce and 2 tablespoons honey. Brush mixture over top of dough.

**6.** Bake 12 to 15 minutes or until lightly browned. Immediately remove from baking sheet; cool on wire rack 10 minutes. Cut into 12 wedges. Serve warm or cool completely.        *Makes 12 servings*

**NUTRIENTS PER SCONE:**

| | |
|---|---|
| Calories | 170 |
| % of Calories from Fat | 13 |
| Total Fat | 3 g |

*Oatmeal Apple Cranberry Scones*

**LIGHT DELIGHTS**

## BLUEBERRY MUFFINS

**1 cup fresh or thawed, frozen blueberries**
**1¾ cups plus 1 tablespoon all-purpose flour, divided**
**2 teaspoons baking powder**
**1 teaspoon grated lemon peel**
**½ teaspoon salt**
**½ cup MOTT'S® Apple Sauce**
**½ cup sugar**
**1 whole egg**
**1 egg white**
**2 tablespoons vegetable oil**
**¼ cup skim milk**

Preheat oven to 375°F. Line 12 (2½-inch) muffin cups with paper liners or spray with nonstick cooking spray.

Toss blueberries with 1 tablespoon flour; set aside. In large bowl, combine remaining 1¾ cups flour, baking powder, lemon peel and salt. Combine apple sauce, sugar, whole egg, egg white and oil; stir into flour mixture alternately with milk. Mix just until moistened. Fold in blueberry mixture. Spoon evenly into prepared muffin cups.

Bake 20 minutes or until toothpick inserted in center comes out clean. Immediately remove from pan; cool on wire rack. *Makes 12 servings*

| NUTRIENTS PER MUFFIN: | |
|---|---|
| Calories | 150 |
| % of Calories from Fat | 18 |
| Total Fat | 3 g |

## BANANA NUT BREAD

**½ cup granulated sugar**
**2 tablespoons brown sugar**
**5 tablespoons margarine**
**1⅓ cups mashed ripe bananas**
**1 egg**
**2 egg whites**
**2½ cups all-purpose flour**
**1 teaspoon baking soda**
**½ teaspoon salt**
**⅓ cup walnuts**

Preheat oven to 375°F. Spray large loaf pan with nonstick cooking spray; set aside. Beat sugars and margarine in large bowl with electric mixer until light and fluffy. Add bananas, egg and egg whites. Sift together flour, baking soda and salt in medium bowl; add to banana mixture. Stir in walnuts. Pour into prepared loaf pan. Bake 1 hour or until wooden pick inserted in center comes out clean. Remove from pan. Cool on wire rack 10 minutes. Serve warm or cool completely.

*Makes 1 loaf (16 servings)*

| NUTRIENTS PER SERVING: | |
|---|---|
| Calories | 174 |
| % of Calories from Fat | 28 |
| Total Fat | 6 g |

*Favorite recipe from **The Sugar Association, Inc.***

*Blueberry Muffins*

## SPICE–PRUNE LOAF

**1 cup chopped pitted prunes**
**½ cup prune juice**
**1 cup all-purpose flour**
**1 cup whole wheat flour**
**1 teaspoon baking powder**
**¾ teaspoon ground cinnamon**
**½ teaspoon baking soda**
**¼ teaspoon ground ginger**
**⅛ teaspoon salt**
**2 egg whites**
**⅓ cup molasses**
**3 tablespoons vegetable oil**
**¼ teaspoon vanilla**

Preheat oven to 350°F. Spray 8×4-inch loaf pan with nonstick cooking spray; set aside. Bring prunes and prune juice to a boil over medium-high heat. Remove from heat; let stand 5 minutes.

Combine flours, baking powder, cinnamon, baking soda, ginger and salt. Stir remaining ingredients into flour mixture just until moistened. Stir in prune mixture.

Pour batter into prepared pan. Bake 55 to 60 minutes or until wooden pick inserted in center comes out clean. Cool completely. Wrap and store overnight at room temperature before slicing.

*Makes 16 servings*

| NUTRIENTS PER SERVING: | |
| --- | --- |
| Calories | 124 |
| % of Calories from Fat | 20 |
| Total Fat | 3 g |

## WILD RICE BLUEBERRY MUFFINS

**1½ cups all-purpose flour**
**½ cup sugar**
**2 teaspoons baking powder**
**1 teaspoon ground cinnamon**
**½ teaspoon salt**
**1 cup fresh blueberries**
**½ cup skim milk**
**¼ cup applesauce**
**4 egg whites**
**1 cup cooked wild rice**

Preheat oven to 400°F. Spray muffin cups with nonstick cooking spray or paper-line. Combine flour, sugar, baking powder, cinnamon and salt in large bowl. Sprinkle 1 tablespoon flour mixture over blueberries; toss to coat. Combine milk, applesauce and egg whites in medium bowl. Fold into batter with blueberries and wild rice. (Batter will be stiff.) Spoon evenly into prepared muffin cups, filling two-thirds full. Bake 15 to 20 minutes or until wooden pick inserted in center comes out clean. Remove from pan. Cool on wire rack 10 minutes. Serve warm or cool completely.

*Makes 12 muffins*

| NUTRIENTS PER MUFFIN: | |
| --- | --- |
| Calories | 120 |
| % of Calories from Fat | 2 |
| Total Fat | <1 g |

*Spice-Prune Loaf*

LIGHT DELIGHTS

## CRANBERRY OAT BRAN MUFFINS

2 cups flour
1 cup oat bran
½ cup packed brown sugar
2 teaspoons baking powder
½ teaspoon baking soda
½ teaspoon salt (optional)
½ cup MIRACLE WHIP® LIGHT Reduced
   Calorie Salad Dressing
3 egg whites, slightly beaten
½ cup skim milk
⅓ cup orange juice
1 teaspoon grated orange peel
1 cup coarsely chopped cranberries

Preheat oven to 375°F. Line 12 medium muffin cups with paper baking cups or spray with nonstick cooking spray. Mix together dry ingredients. Add combined dressing, egg whites, milk, juice and peel; mix just until moistened. Fold in cranberries. Fill prepared muffin cups almost full. Bake 15 to 17 minutes or until golden brown.

*Makes 12 muffins*

### NUTRIENTS PER MUFFIN:

| | |
|---|---|
| Calories | 183 |
| % of Calories from Fat | 20 |
| Total Fat | 4 g |

## APPLE OAT BRAN MUFFINS

¾ cup unsifted all-purpose flour
¾ cup whole wheat flour
1½ teaspoons ground cinnamon
1 teaspoon baking powder
½ teaspoon baking soda
¼ teaspoon salt
1 cup buttermilk
½ cup oat bran
¼ cup packed brown sugar
2 tablespoons vegetable oil
1 large egg
1½ cups Golden Delicious apples, peeled,
   cored and finely diced

**1.** Heat oven to 400°F. Grease 12 muffin cups or fill with paper muffin-cup liners. In large bowl, combine flours, cinnamon, baking powder, baking soda and salt. In medium-size bowl, beat together buttermilk, oat bran, sugar, oil and egg. Add buttermilk mixture to flour mixture, stirring until just combined; fold in apples.

**2.** Divide batter among prepared muffin cups. Bake 18 to 20 minutes or until wooden pick inserted in centers comes out clean. Cool muffins 5 minutes in pan; remove from pan and cool on wire rack.

*Makes 12 muffins*

### NUTRIENTS PER MUFFIN:

| | |
|---|---|
| Calories | 121 |
| % of Calories from Fat | 22 |
| Total Fat | 3 g |

*Favorite recipe from* **Washington Apple Commission**

*Cranberry Oat Bran Muffins*

LIGHT DELIGHTS

## CHIVE WHOLE WHEAT DROP BISCUITS

**1¼ cups whole wheat flour**
**¾ cup all-purpose flour**
**3 tablespoons toasted wheat germ, divided**
**1 tablespoon baking powder**
**1 tablespoon chopped fresh chives *or***
    **1 teaspoon dried chives**
**2 teaspoons sugar**
**3 tablespoons margarine**
**1 cup skim milk**
**½ cup shredded low fat process American cheese**

Preheat oven to 450°F. Spray baking sheet with nonstick cooking spray; set aside. Combine flours, 2 tablespoons wheat germ, baking powder, chives and sugar in medium bowl. Cut in margarine with pastry blender until mixture resembles coarse crumbs. Add milk and cheese; stir just until moistened.

Drop rounded teaspoonfuls of dough 1 inch apart onto prepared baking sheet. Sprinkle remaining 1 tablespoon wheat germ over tops of biscuits. Bake 10 to 12 minutes or until golden brown and wooden pick inserted in center comes out clean. Remove immediately from baking sheet.

*Makes 12 servings*

**NUTRIENTS PER BISCUIT:**

| | |
|---|---|
| Calories | 125 |
| % of Calories from Fat | 28 |
| Total Fat | 4 g |

## BLUEBERRY CRUNCH MUFFINS

**¾ cup skim milk**
**3 tablespoons vegetable oil**
**1 egg**
**1¼ cups all-purpose flour**
**½ cup whole wheat flour**
**½ cup packed brown sugar**
**¼ cup uncooked rolled oats**
**¼ cup granulated sugar**
**2 teaspoons baking powder**
**¼ teaspoon salt**
**⅛ teaspoon ground cinnamon**
**1 cup fresh or frozen blueberries, thawed, drained**
**Crunch Topping (recipe follows)**

Preheat oven to 400°F. Spray muffin cups or loaf pan with nonstick cooking spray; set aside. In food processor or large bowl combine milk, oil and egg; process until smooth. Combine flours, brown sugar, oats, granulated sugar, baking powder, salt and cinnamon in medium bowl. Stir into milk mixture just until moistened. Fold in blueberries. Spoon evenly into prepared muffin cups. Sprinkle Crunch Topping over top of each muffin. Bake muffins 15 to 18 minutes (25 to 30 minutes for loaf) or until golden brown and wooden pick inserted in center comes out clean. Remove from pan. Cool on wire rack 10 minutes. Serve warm or cool completely. *Makes about 18 small muffins or 1 loaf*

## LIGHT DELIGHTS

**CRUNCH TOPPING:** Blend ¼ cup whole wheat breakfast cereal flakes, 1 tablespoon flour, 2 tablespoons granulated sugar and 1 teaspoon butter in food processor.

| NUTRIENTS PER MUFFIN: | |
|---|---|
| Calories | 114 |
| % of Calories from Fat | 22 |
| Total Fat | 3 g |

**PUMPKIN VARIATION:** Omit blueberries. *Decrease* milk to ½ cup. Fold ¾ cup canned pumpkin, ⅛ teaspoon nutmeg, 2 tablespoons walnut pieces into batter.

*Favorite recipe from* **The Sugar Association, Inc.**

## MINI MUFFINS

 2 ripe bananas *or* 8 ounces solid pack
  pumpkin
 1 cup packed brown sugar
 2 egg whites
 2 tablespoons vegetable oil
 1¼ cups all-purpose flour
 ¾ cup whole wheat flour
 2 teaspoons baking powder
 ½ teaspoon baking soda
 ½ teaspoon ground cinnamon
 1 tablespoon granulated sugar
  Peach Spread (recipe follows)

Preheat oven to 400°F. Spray mini-muffin cups with cooking spray; set aside. In large bowl mash bananas. Combine brown sugar, egg whites and oil until well blended; add to bananas. Combine flours, baking powder, baking soda, cinnamon and granulated sugar in medium bowl. Stir into banana mixture just until moistened. Let stand 5 minutes. Spoon evenly into prepared muffin cups, filling half full. Sprinkle additional granulated sugar over top of each muffin. Bake 15 to 18 minutes or until golden brown and wooden pick inserted in center comes out clean. Remove from pans. Cool on wire racks 10 minutes. Serve with Peach Spread.

*Makes about 48 mini muffins*

Peach Spread
 ½ **cup frozen peaches, thawed, drained**
 ¼ **cup part-skim ricotta cheese**
 2 **tablespoons powdered sugar**

In food processor combine all ingredients; process until smooth. *Makes 30 servings*

| NUTRIENTS PER MINI MUFFIN: | |
|---|---|
| Calories | 55 |
| % of Calories from Fat | 13 |
| Fat | <1 g |

*Favorite recipe from* **The Sugar Association, Inc.**

*— Sweet —*

# SNACKIN' TREATS

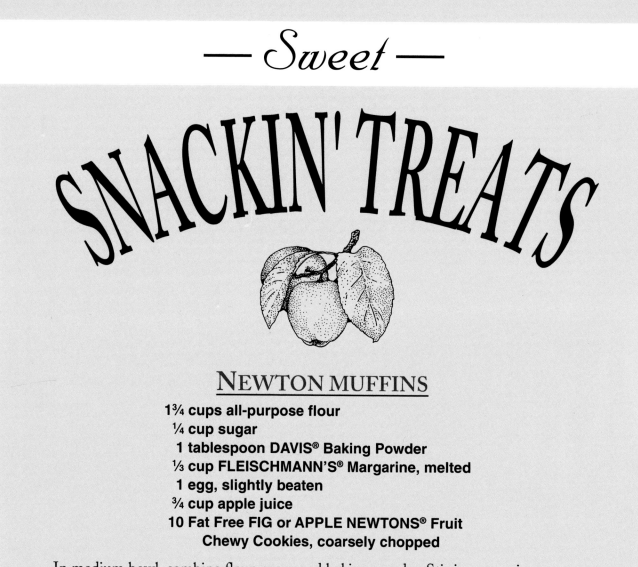

## NEWTON MUFFINS

1¾ cups all-purpose flour
¼ cup sugar
1 tablespoon DAVIS® Baking Powder
⅓ cup FLEISCHMANN'S® Margarine, melted
1 egg, slightly beaten
¾ cup apple juice
10 Fat Free FIG or APPLE NEWTONS® Fruit
Chewy Cookies, coarsely chopped

In medium bowl, combine flour, sugar and baking powder. Stir in margarine, egg and apple juice just until blended. (Batter will be lumpy.) Stir in cookies. Fill 12 greased 2½-inch muffin-pan cups.

Bake at 400°F for 15 to 20 minutes or until toothpick inserted in center comes out clean. Serve warm or cold.                                    *Makes 1 dozen muffins*

SNACKIN' TREATS

# GINGERBREAD PEAR MUFFINS

1¾ cups all-purpose flour
⅓ cup sugar
2 teaspoons baking powder
¾ teaspoon ground ginger
¼ teaspoon baking soda
¼ teaspoon salt
¼ teaspoon ground cinnamon
1 medium pear
⅓ cup milk
¼ cup vegetable oil
¼ cup light molasses
1 egg

1. Preheat oven to 375°F. Grease or paper-line 12 (2½-inch) muffin cups; set aside.

2. Sift flour, sugar, baking powder, ginger, baking soda, salt and cinnamon into large bowl.

3. Peel pear with vegetable peeler. Cut pear lengthwise into halves, then into quarters with utility knife; remove core and seeds.

4. Finely chop pear with chef's knife to measure 1 cup.

5. Combine milk, oil, molasses and egg in medium bowl until well blended; stir in pear. Stir into flour mixture just until moistened.

6. Spoon evenly into prepared muffin cups, filling two-thirds full.

7. Bake 20 minutes or until wooden pick inserted in center comes out clean. Remove from pan. Cool on wire rack 10 minutes. Serve warm or cool completely. *Makes 12 muffins*

# QUICK NECTARINE OAT MUFFINS

2 cups whole wheat flour
3 fresh California nectarines, finely chopped (2 cups)
1½ cups buttermilk
1 cup uncooked rolled oats
½ cup unprocessed bran
½ cup packed brown sugar
¼ cup vegetable oil
2 eggs
1 tablespoon grated orange peel
1½ teaspoons baking soda
1½ teaspoons ground cinnamon
1 teaspoon salt

Preheat oven to 400°F. Grease 20 (2½-inch) muffin cups; set aside. Combine all ingredients in mixing bowl just until moistened. Spoon evenly into prepared muffin cups. Bake 20 minutes or until wooden pick inserted in center comes out clean. Remove from pans. Cool on wire racks 10 minutes. Serve warm or cool completely.

*Makes 20 muffins*

*Favorite recipe from* **California Tree Fruit Agreement**

*Gingerbread Pear Muffins*

SNACKIN' TREATS

# ALMOND BRIOCHES

**1 package active dry yeast**
**⅓ cup plus 1 teaspoon sugar, divided**
**½ cup warm water (105° to 115°F)**
**½ cup butter or margarine, softened**
**3 eggs**
**½ teaspoon almond extract**
**3½ cups all-purpose flour, divided**
**¾ teaspoon salt**
**¼ cup packed almond paste (about 2 ounces), cut into 16 pieces and flattened into nickel-size discs**
**1 egg yolk**
**1 tablespoon half-and-half or milk**
**¼ cup sliced almonds**
**Additional sugar (optional)**

To proof yeast, sprinkle yeast and 1 teaspoon sugar over warm water in small bowl; stir until yeast is dissolved. Let stand 5 minutes or until mixture is bubbly. Beat butter and ⅓ cup sugar in large bowl with electric mixer at medium speed until light and fluffy. Add eggs, one at a time, beating well and scraping down side of bowl after each addition. Beat in almond extract. Reduce speed to low; beat in yeast mixture, 1½ cups flour and salt. Beat at medium speed 2 minutes. Stir in remaining 2 cups flour with wooden spoon. Continue stirring about 5 minutes. Dough will be sticky.

Cover with towel; let rise in warm place about 1½ hours or until doubled in bulk. Stir down dough with wooden spoon. Cover with plastic wrap; refrigerate 2 hours or overnight. Punch down

dough. Turn out dough onto lightly floured surface; flatten slightly. Knead dough 2 minutes. Cut dough into 16 pieces. Cover with towel; let rest 10 minutes. Grease 16 (3¾×1½-inch) brioche pans or 16 (2½-inch) muffin pan cups; set aside.

To form brioches, reserve about 1 teaspoon dough from each piece, shaping larger pieces of dough into balls. Pull edges of each dough piece under and around almond paste disc, making smooth round top. Continue pulling dough under until piece is evenly shaped. Place in prepared pans. (Overhandling makes dough warm and sticky and hard to shape. If dough becomes too soft and sticky, refrigerate 10 minutes.) To form top knot, make deep depression in each dough ball with a greased end of wooden spoon. Shape small dough piece into tear-drop-shaped ball; place pointed end of ball into hole. Repeat with remaining dough. Place brioche pans on jelly-roll pan. Cover brioches with towel; let rise in warm place 45 minutes or until almost doubled in bulk.

Preheat oven to 375°F. Combine egg yolk and half-and-half in small bowl. Brush brioches with egg yolk mixture. Sprinkle with almonds and additional sugar, if desired. Bake 20 minutes or until brioches are golden and sound hollow when lightly tapped. Remove from pans; cool on wire racks 10 minutes. Serve warm.

*Makes 16 brioches*

*Almond Brioche*

SNACKIN' TREATS

## STREUSEL–TOPPED BLUEBERRY MUFFINS

**1½ cups plus ⅓ cup all-purpose flour, divided**
**½ cup plus ⅓ cup sugar, divided**
**1 teaspoon ground cinnamon**
**3 tablespoons butter or margarine, cut into small pieces**
**2 teaspoons baking powder**
**½ teaspoon salt**
**1 cup milk**
**¼ cup butter or margarine, melted and slightly cooled**
**1 egg, beaten**
**1 teaspoon vanilla**
**1 cup fresh blueberries**

Preheat oven to 375°F. Grease or paper-line 12 (2½-inch) muffin cups; set aside.

Combine ⅓ cup flour, ⅓ cup sugar and cinnamon in small bowl; mix well. Cut in 3 tablespoons butter with pastry blender or 2 knives until mixture resembles coarse crumbs; set aside for topping.

Combine remaining 1½ cups flour, ½ cup sugar, baking powder and salt in large bowl. Combine milk, ¼ cup melted butter, egg and vanilla in small bowl until well blended. Stir into flour mixture just until moistened. (Do not overmix.) Fold in blueberries. Spoon evenly into prepared muffin cups. Sprinkle reserved topping over top of each muffin.

Bake 20 to 25 minutes or until wooden pick inserted in center comes out clean. Remove from pan. Cool on wire rack 10 minutes. Serve warm or cool completely. *Makes 12 muffins*

## MINT CHOCOLATE CHIP MUFFINS

**2⅓ cups all-purpose flour**
**1¼ cups sugar**
**⅓ cup unsweetened cocoa powder**
**2 teaspoons baking powder**
**1 teaspoon baking soda**
**½ teaspoon salt**
**1 cup sour cream**
**⅓ cup butter or margarine, melted**
**¼ cup milk**
**2 eggs, beaten**
**1 cup mint flavored semi-sweet chocolate chips**

Preheat oven to 400°F. Grease 12 (3½-inch) large muffin cups; set aside. Combine flour, sugar, cocoa, baking powder, baking soda and salt in large bowl. Combine sour cream, butter, milk and eggs in small bowl until blended. Stir into flour mixture just until moistened. Fold in mint chips. Spoon into prepared muffin cups, filling half full. Bake 25 to 30 minutes or until wooden pick inserted in center comes out clean. Cool in pan 5 minutes. Remove from pan. Cool on wire rack 10 minutes. Serve warm or cool completely.

*Makes 12 jumbo muffins*

*Streusel-Topped Blueberry Muffins*

SNACKIN' TREATS

## BAKED DOUGHNUTS WITH CINNAMON GLAZE

**5 to 5½ cups all-purpose flour, divided**
**⅔ cup granulated sugar**
**2 packages active dry yeast**
**1 teaspoon salt**
**1 teaspoon grated lemon peel**
**½ teaspoon ground nutmeg**
**2 cups milk, divided**
**½ cup butter or margarine**
**2 eggs**
**2 cups sifted powdered sugar**
**½ teaspoon ground cinnamon**

Combine 2 cups flour, granulated sugar, yeast, salt, lemon peel and nutmeg in large bowl. Combine 1¾ cups milk and butter in 1-quart saucepan. Heat over low heat until mixture is 120° to 130°F. (Butter does not need to completely melt.) Gradually beat milk mixture into flour mixture with electric mixer at low speed. Increase speed to medium; beat 2 minutes. Beat in eggs and 1 cup flour at low speed. Increase speed to medium; beat 2 minutes. Stir in enough additional flour, about 2 cups, to make soft dough. Cover with plastic wrap; refrigerate at least 2 hours or up to 24 hours.

Punch down dough. Turn out dough onto lightly floured surface. Knead dough about 1 minute or until dough is no longer sticky, adding ½ cup flour to prevent sticking if necessary. Grease 2 large baking sheets. Roll out dough to ½-inch thickness with lightly floured rolling pin. Cut dough with floured 2¾-inch doughnut cutter. Reroll scraps, reserving doughnut holes. Place doughnuts and holes 2 inches apart on prepared baking sheets. Cover with towel and let rise in warm place about 30 minutes or until doubled in bulk.

Preheat oven to 400°F. To prepare glaze, combine powdered sugar and cinnamon in small bowl. Stir in enough remaining milk, about ¼ cup, to thin glaze to desired consistency. Cover; set aside.

Bake doughnuts and holes 8 to 10 minutes or until golden brown. Remove from pan with spatula; cool on wire racks 5 minutes. Dip tops of warm doughnuts into glaze. Place right side up on racks, allowing glaze to drip down sides. Best when served warm.

*Makes 2 dozen doughnuts and holes*

*Baked Doughnuts with Cinnamon Glaze*

SNACKIN' TREATS

## CHOCOLATE PUMPKIN MUFFINS

**1½ cups all-purpose flour**
**½ cup granulated sugar**
**2 teaspoons baking powder**
**½ teaspoon ground cinnamon**
**½ teaspoon salt**
**1 cup milk**
**½ cup LIBBY'S® Solid Pack Pumpkin**
**¼ cup margarine or butter, melted**
**1 egg**
**1 cup (6-ounce package) NESTLÉ® TOLL HOUSE® Semi-Sweet Chocolate Morsels**
**⅓ cup finely chopped nuts**

Preheat oven to 400°F. Grease 12 (2½-inch) muffin cups.

In large bowl, combine flour, sugar, baking powder, cinnamon and salt; make well in center. In small bowl, combine milk, pumpkin, margarine and egg; add to well in flour mixture. Add morsels; stir just until dry ingredients are moistened. Spoon into prepared muffin cups, filling each ¾ full. Sprinkle 1 teaspoon nuts over each muffin.

Bake 18 to 20 minutes or until wooden pick inserted into center comes out clean. Cool 5 minutes; remove from pans. Cool completely on wire racks.     *Makes 12 muffins*

## HONEY MUFFINS

**2 cups all-purpose flour**
**¼ cup sugar**
**2 teaspoons baking powder**
**1 teaspoon baking soda**
**½ teaspoon salt**
**½ cup honey**
**½ cup orange juice**
**⅓ cup butter or margarine, melted**
**2 eggs, beaten**
**1 teaspoon vanilla**

Preheat oven to 375°F. Grease 12 muffin cups; set aside.

Combine flour, sugar, baking powder, baking soda and salt in large bowl. Combine honey, orange juice, butter, eggs and vanilla in medium bowl until well blended. Stir into flour mixture just until blended. Spoon evenly into prepared muffin cups, filling two-thirds full. Bake 15 to 20 minutes or until golden brown and wooden pick inserted in center comes out clean. Remove from pan. Cool on wire rack 10 minutes. Serve warm or cool completely.     *Makes 12 muffins*

**TIP:** To make giant muffins, spoon batter equally into 5 giant muffin tins. Bake at 350°F 25 to 30 minutes or until golden.

*Favorite recipe from **National Honey Board***

*Chocolate Pumpkin Muffins*

## IRISH SODA BREAD

**4 cups all-purpose flour**
**¼ cup sugar**
**1 tablespoon baking powder**
**1 teaspoon baking soda**
**1 teaspoon salt**
**1 tablespoon caraway seeds**
**⅓ cup vegetable shortening**
**1 cup raisins or currants**
**1 egg**
**1¾ cups buttermilk***
**Additional sugar (optional)**

*Or, substitute soured fresh milk. To sour milk, place 2 tablespoons lemon juice *plus* enough milk to equal 1¾ cups in 2-cup measure. Stir; let stand 5 minutes before using.

Preheat oven to 350°F. Grease large baking sheet; set aside. Sift flour, ¼ cup sugar, baking powder, baking soda and salt into large bowl. Stir in caraway seeds. Cut in shortening with pastry blender or 2 knives until mixture resembles coarse crumbs. Stir in raisins. Beat egg in medium bowl using fork. Add buttermilk; beat until well combined. Add buttermilk mixture to flour mixture; stir until mixture forms soft dough that clings together and forms a ball. Turn out dough onto well-floured surface. Knead dough gently 10 to 12 times. Place dough on prepared baking sheet. Pat dough into 7-inch round. Score top of dough with tip of sharp knife, making an "X" about 4 inches long and ¼ inch deep.

Bake 55 to 60 minutes or until wooden toothpick inserted in center comes out clean. Immediately remove from baking sheet; cool on wire rack.** Bread is best eaten the day it is made.

*Makes 12 servings*

**For a sweet crust, combine 1 tablespoon sugar and 1 tablespoon water in custard cup. Brush over hot loaf.

## HONEY SHORTBREAD

**1 cup butter**
**⅓ cup honey**
**1 teaspoon vanilla**
**2½ cups all-purpose flour**
**¾ cup chopped pecans**

Preheat oven to 300°F. Beat butter, honey and vanilla in medium bowl with electric mixer until light and fluffy. Add flour, 1 cup at a time, beating well after each addition. (If dough becomes too stiff to stir, knead in remaining flour by hand.) Stir in nuts with spoon. Pat dough into shortbread mold or ungreased 9-inch cast iron skillet. Score surface of dough into 24 wedges with knife. Prick deeply into knife scores with fork. Bake 35 to 40 minutes or until wooden pick inserted in center comes out clean. Cool in mold 10 minutes. Remove from mold. Cut into wedges. Serve warm or cool completely.      *Makes 24 wedges*

*Favorite recipe from **National Honey Board***

*Irish Soda Bread*

SNACKIN' TREATS

## GLAZED STRAWBERRY LEMON STREUSEL MUFFINS

**Lemon Streusel Topping (recipe follows)**
**Lemony Glaze (recipe follows)**
1½ **cups all-purpose flour**
½ **cup sugar**
2 **teaspoons baking powder**
1 **teaspoon ground cinnamon**
¼ **teaspoon salt**
½ **cup milk**
½ **cup butter or margarine, melted**
1 **egg**
1½ **cups fresh strawberries, chopped**
1 **teaspoon grated lemon peel**

Preheat oven to 375°F. Paper-line 12 (2½-inch) muffin cups. Prepare Lemon Streusel Topping and Lemony Glaze; set aside.

Combine flour, sugar, baking powder, cinnamon and salt in large bowl. Combine milk, butter and egg in small bowl until well blended. Stir into flour mixture just until moistened. Fold in strawberries and lemon peel. Spoon evenly into prepared muffin cups. Sprinkle Lemon Streusel Topping evenly over tops of muffins.

Bake 20 to 25 minutes or until wooden pick inserted in center comes out clean. Remove from pan. Cool on wire rack 10 minutes. Drizzle Lemony Glaze over tops of warm muffins. Serve warm or cool completely.          *Makes 12 muffins*

**LEMON STREUSEL TOPPING:** Combine ¼ cup chopped pecans, ¼ cup packed brown sugar, 2 tablespoons all-purpose flour, ½ teaspoon ground cinnamon and ½ teaspoon grated lemon peel in medium bowl. Add 1 tablespoon melted butter or margarine, stirring until crumbly.

**LEMONY GLAZE:** Combine ½ cup powdered sugar and 1 tablespoon fresh lemon juice in small bowl, stirring until smooth.

## GOLDEN APPLE SOUR CREAM MUFFINS

1 **cup dairy sour cream**
1 **egg, beaten**
3 **tablespoons sugar**
2 **tablespoons vegetable oil**
1½ **cups flour**
1 **teaspoon baking powder**
½ **teaspoon salt**
¼ **teaspoon baking soda**
⅛ **teaspoon ground allspice**
½ **cup currants or raisins**
1 **cup chopped Golden Delicious apple**

Combine sour cream, egg, sugar and oil. Combine flour, baking powder, salt, baking soda and allspice; stir into sour cream mixture. Fold in currants and apple. Spoon evenly into 12 greased muffin cups. Bake at 400°F 20 to 25 minutes or until wooden pick inserted near center comes out clean.
*Makes 12 muffins*

*Favorite recipe from* **Washington Apple Commission**

*Glazed Strawberry Lemon Streusel Muffins*

**SNACKIN' TREATS**

# CINNAMON–RAISIN BREAD

**1 package active dry yeast**
**½ cup plus 1 teaspoon sugar, divided**
**¼ cup warm water (105° to 115°F)**
**2 eggs, divided**
**3 to 3½ cups all-purpose flour, divided**
**1 teaspoon salt**
**⅔ cup warm milk (105° to 115°F)**
**3 tablespoons butter or margarine, softened**
**1 teaspoon vanilla**
**¾ cup raisins**
**1 tablespoon ground cinnamon**
**1 tablespoon butter or margarine, melted**
**1 tablespoon water**

To proof yeast, sprinkle yeast and 1 teaspoon sugar over warm water in small bowl; stir until yeast is dissolved. Let stand 5 minutes or until mixture is bubbly. Separate 1 egg. Place yolk in another bowl; set aside. Cover white with plastic wrap; store in refrigerator until needed.

Combine 1½ cups flour, ¼ cup sugar and salt in large bowl. Gradually beat yeast mixture, warm milk and softened butter into flour mixture with electric mixer at low speed. Increase speed to medium; beat 2 minutes. Reduce speed to low. Beat in remaining whole egg, reserved egg yolk and vanilla. Increase speed to medium; beat 2 minutes, scraping down side of bowl once. Stir in raisins and enough additional flour, about 1½ cups, with wooden spoon to make soft dough. Turn out dough onto lightly floured surface; flatten slightly. Knead dough about 5 minutes or until smooth and elastic, adding ½ cup more flour to prevent sticking, if necessary. Dough will be soft and slightly sticky.

Shape dough into a ball; place in large greased bowl. Turn dough over so that top is greased. Cover with towel; let rise in warm place 1 to 1½ hours or until doubled in bulk. Punch down dough. Knead dough on lightly floured surface 1 minute. Cover with towel; let rest 10 minutes. Grease 9×5-inch loaf pan; set aside. Combine remaining ¼ cup sugar and cinnamon. Place 1 tablespoon mixture in small cup; set aside.

Roll dough into 20×9-inch rectangle with lightly floured rolling pin. Brush with 1 tablespoon melted butter. Sprinkle ¼ cup cinnamon mixture evenly over butter. Starting with 1 (9-inch) side, roll up dough jelly-roll fashion. Pinch ends and seam to seal. Place loaf, seam side down, in prepared pan, tucking ends under. Cover with towel; let rise in warm place about 1¼ hours or until doubled in bulk. (Dough should rise to top of pan.)

Preheat oven to 350°F. Combine reserved egg white and 1 tablespoon water in small bowl. Brush loaf with egg white mixture; sprinkle with reserved 1 tablespoon cinnamon mixture.

Bake 40 to 45 minutes or until loaf sounds hollow when tapped. Immediately remove from pan; cool completely on wire rack. *Makes 1 loaf*

*Cinnamon-Raisin Bread*

SNACKIN' TREATS

## CINNAMON APPLE TEA BREAD

**1¼ cups boiling water**
**4 LIPTON® Soothing Moments Cinnamon Apple Herbal Tea Bags**
**½ cup raisins**
**½ cup honey**
**2 tablespoons margarine or butter**
**1 egg**
**3 cups all-purpose flour**
**1 tablespoon baking powder**
**½ teaspoon salt**
**½ cup chopped walnuts or pecans**
**2 tablespoons honey**
**½ cup confectioners' sugar**

Preheat oven to 350°F. In teapot, pour boiling water over cinnamon apple herbal tea bags; cover and steep 5 minutes. Remove tea bags and reserve 2 tablespoons tea.

In large bowl, pour remaining tea over raisins, ½ cup honey and margarine and cool completely. Beat in egg.

In medium bowl, combine flour, baking powder and salt. Gradually add to tea mixture, blending well after each addition. Stir in walnuts.

Spoon into greased and floured 9×5×3-inch loaf pan and bake 1 hour or until wooden pick inserted in center comes out clean. On wire rack, cool 10 minutes; remove from pan and cool completely before glazing.

Meanwhile, in small bowl, gradually add enough reserved tea and 2 tablespoons honey to confectioners' sugar until desired thickness; drizzle over bread.      *Makes about 8 servings*

## IN–THE–CHIPS CARROT MUFFINS

**12 CHIPS AHOY!® Chocolate Chip Cookies, finely rolled (about 1¼ cups crumbs)**
**1 cup all-purpose flour**
**1 cup grated carrots**
**⅓ cup walnuts, chopped**
**3 tablespoons firmly packed light brown sugar**
**1 tablespoon DAVIS® Baking Powder**
**1 egg**
**¾ cup milk**
**¼ cup margarine, melted**
**Soft cream cheese, optional**

In medium bowl, combine cookie crumbs, flour, carrots, walnuts, brown sugar and baking powder; set aside.

In small bowl, blend egg, milk and margarine; stir into flour mixture just until moistened. Spoon into 12 greased 2½-inch muffin-pan cups.

Bake at 400°F for 20 to 25 minutes or until toothpick inserted in center comes out clean. Cool slightly; serve topped with cream cheese, if desired.
*Makes 12 muffins*

SNACKIN' TREATS

**MICROWAVE DIRECTIONS:** Prepare batter as above. In each of 6 microwavable muffin-pan cups, place 2 paper liners. Spoon batter into cups, filling ²⁄₃ full. Microwave on HIGH (100% power) for 2½ to 3½ minutes or until toothpick inserted in center comes out clean, rotating dish ½ turn after 1 minute. Let stand 1 minute on heatproof surface; remove to rack. Repeat with remaining batter.

## GERMAN CHOCOLATE MUFFINS

**German Chocolate Topping (recipe follows)**
**1 package (18.25 ounces) pudding-included German chocolate cake mix, plus ingredients to prepare mix**

Preheat oven to 400°F. Grease 12 (3½-inch) large muffin cups; set aside. Prepare German Chocolate Topping; set aside.

Prepare cake mix according to package directions, *reducing* water by ¼ cup. Spoon into prepared muffin cups, filling half full. Sprinkle German Chocolate Topping evenly over tops of muffins.

Bake 20 to 25 minutes or until wooden pick inserted in center comes out clean. Cool in pan on wire rack 5 minutes. Remove from pan. Cool on wire rack 10 minutes. Serve warm or cool completely. *Makes 12 jumbo muffins*

**GERMAN CHOCOLATE TOPPING:**
Combine 3 tablespoons *each* chopped pecans, flaked coconut and packed brown sugar in small bowl.

## PLUM OAT SQUARES

**1 cup uncooked rolled oats**
**⅓ cup whole wheat flour**
**⅓ cup packed brown sugar**
**1 teaspoon ground cinnamon**
**¼ teaspoon baking soda**
**¼ teaspoon ground nutmeg**
**1 egg, slightly beaten**
**2 tablespoons unsalted butter, melted**
**2 tablespoons unsweetened apple juice concentrate, thawed**
**1 teaspoon vanilla**
**2 fresh California plums, finely chopped**

Preheat oven to 350°F. Grease 11×7-inch baking pan; set aside. Combine oats, flour, sugar, cinnamon, baking soda and nutmeg in large bowl. Combine egg, butter, juice and vanilla in small bowl until well blended. Stir into oat mixture until well blended. Fold in plums. Spread evenly into prepared pan. Bake 25 minutes or until wooden pick inserted in center comes out clean. Cool in pan on wire rack 10 minutes. Cut into squares. Serve warm or cool completely.

*Makes 12 squares*

*Favorite recipe from* **California Tree Fruit Agreement**

SNACKIN' TREATS

## LEMON POPPY SEED MUFFINS

  3 cups all-purpose flour
  1 cup sugar
  3 tablespoons poppy seeds
  1 tablespoon grated lemon peel
  2 teaspoons baking powder
  1 teaspoon baking soda
  ½ teaspoon salt
  1 container (16 ounces) low fat plain yogurt
  ½ cup fresh lemon juice
  ¼ cup vegetable oil
  2 eggs, beaten
  1½ teaspoons vanilla

Preheat oven to 400°F. Grease 12 (3½-inch) large muffin cups; set aside.

Combine flour, sugar, poppy seeds, lemon peel, baking powder, baking soda and salt in large bowl. Combine yogurt, lemon juice, oil, eggs and vanilla in small bowl until well blended. Stir into flour mixture just until moistened. Spoon into prepared muffin cups, filling two-thirds full.

Bake 25 to 30 minutes or until wooden pick inserted in center comes out clean. Cool in pans on wire racks 5 minutes. Remove from pans. Cool on wire racks 10 minutes. Serve warm or cool completely. *Makes 12 jumbo muffins*

## MINI CRUMBCAKES

  2 cups (12-ounce package) NESTLÉ® TOLL HOUSE® Semi-Sweet Chocolate Mini Morsels, divided
  2 cups all-purpose flour
  3 tablespoons granulated sugar
  1 tablespoon baking powder
  ¼ teaspoon salt
  ½ cup (1 stick) butter, melted
  ⅔ cup milk
  2 eggs
  1 teaspoon vanilla extract
  Topping (recipe follows)

**Combine** 1½ cups morsels, flour, sugar, baking powder and salt in large bowl. Combine butter, milk, eggs and vanilla in small bowl; add to flour mixture and stir just until moistened.

**Spoon** batter into greased or paper-lined muffin cups, filling about ¾ full. Sprinkle with Topping.

**Bake** in preheated 400°F. oven for 18 to 20 minutes or until wooden pick inserted in center comes out clean. Let stand for 5 minutes on wire racks. Remove from pans to wire racks to cool completely. *Makes 18 crumbcakes*

**Topping: Combine** ½ cup chopped walnuts, ⅓ cup packed brown sugar, 2 tablespoons butter, melted and 1 tablespoon all-purpose flour in small bowl; stir in remaining morsels.

*Lemon Poppy Seed Muffins*

## PEANUT BUTTER MINI CHIP LOAVES

   **3 cups all-purpose flour**
**1½ teaspoons baking powder**
   **1 teaspoon baking soda**
   **1 teaspoon salt**
   **1 cup creamy peanut butter**
  **½ cup butter or margarine, softened**
  **½ cup granulated sugar**
  **½ cup light brown sugar**
   **2 eggs**
**1½ cups buttermilk***
   **2 teaspoons vanilla**
   **1 cup mini semisweet chocolate chips**

*Or, substitute soured fresh milk. To sour milk, place 1½ tablespoons lemon juice *plus* enough milk to equal 1½ cups in 2-cup measure. Stir; let stand 5 minutes before using.

Preheat oven to 350°F. Grease 2 (8½×4½-inch) loaf pans. Sift flour, baking powder, baking soda and salt into large bowl; set aside.

Beat peanut butter, butter, granulated sugar and brown sugar in large bowl with electric mixer at medium speed until light and fluffy. Beat in eggs, one at a time, scraping down side of bowl after each addition. Beat in buttermilk and vanilla. Gradually add flour mixture. Beat at low speed. Stir in chips with wooden spoon. Spoon into prepared pans.

Bake 45 minutes or until wooden toothpick inserted in center comes out clean. Cool in pans on wire rack 10 minutes. Remove from pans; cool completely on rack. *Makes 2 loaves*

## OREO® MUFFINS

**1¾ cups all-purpose flour**
  **½ cup sugar**
  **1 tablespoon DAVIS® Baking Powder**
  **½ teaspoon salt**
  **¾ cup milk**
  **⅓ cup sour cream**
  **1 egg**
  **¼ cup margarine, melted**
**20 OREO® Chocolate Sandwich Cookies, coarsely chopped**

In medium bowl, combine flour, sugar, baking powder and salt; set aside.

In small bowl, combine milk, sour cream and egg; stir into flour mixture with margarine until just blended. Gently stir in cookies. Spoon batter into 12 greased 2½-inch muffin-pan cups.

Bake at 400°F for 20 to 25 minutes or until toothpick inserted in center comes out clean. Remove from pan; cool on wire rack. Serve warm or cold. *Makes 1 dozen muffins*

*Peanut Butter Mini Chip Loaves*

SNACKIN' TREATS

## CHOCOLATE POPOVERS

**¾ cup plus 2 tablespoons all-purpose flour**
**¼ cup granulated sugar**
**2 tablespoons unsweetened cocoa powder**
**¼ teaspoon salt**
**4 eggs**
**1 cup milk**
**2 tablespoons butter or margarine, melted**
**½ teaspoon vanilla**
**Powdered sugar**

**1.** Position rack in lower third of oven. Preheat oven to 375°F. Grease 6-cup popover pan or 6 (6-ounce) custard cups. Set custard cups in jelly-roll pan for easier handling.

**2.** Sift flour, granulated sugar, cocoa and salt into medium bowl; set aside.

**3.** Beat eggs in large bowl with electric mixer at low speed 1 minute. Beat in milk, butter and vanilla. Beat in flour mixture until smooth.

**4.** Pour batter into prepared pan. Bake 50 minutes.

**5.** Place pieces of waxed paper under wire rack to keep counter clean.

**6.** Immediately remove popovers to wire rack. Place powdered sugar in fine-mesh sieve. Generously sprinkle powdered sugar over popovers. Serve immediately.  *Makes 6 popovers*

## PUMPKIN PECAN NUT BREAD

**1 cup solid pack pumpkin**
**½ cup sugar**
**½ cup buttermilk**
**1 egg**
**1½ cups sifted all-purpose flour**
**1¼ teaspoons baking soda**
**1 teaspoon salt**
**½ teaspoon ground cinnamon**
**¼ teaspoon ground ginger**
**⅛ teaspoon ground cloves**
**2 tablespoons butter, softened**
**1 cup chopped pecans**

Preheat oven to 350°F. Grease loaf pan; set aside. Combine pumpkin, sugar, buttermilk and egg in large bowl. Sift flour, baking soda, salt and spices into medium bowl. Stir into pumpkin mixture with butter until well blended. Stir in pecans. Pour into prepared loaf pan. Bake 1 hour or until wooden pick inserted in center comes out clean. Remove from pan. Cool on wire rack 10 minutes. Serve warm or cool completely.  *Makes 1 loaf*

**FOR MUFFINS:** Spoon evenly into greased muffin cups. Bake 25 to 35 minutes or until wooden pick inserted in center comes out clean. Remove from pan. Cool on wire rack 10 minutes. Serve warm or cool completely.

*Favorite recipe from* **Pecan Marketing Board**

*Chocolate Popovers*

## SNACKIN' TREATS

## SPICY PLUM MUFFINS

**4 fresh California plums, chopped**
**1 cup sugar**
**½ cup vegetable oil or melted margarine**
**1 egg**
**1½ cups all-purpose flour**
**½ cup oat bran**
**2 teaspoons baking soda**
**2 teaspoons ground cinnamon**
**½ teaspoon ground cloves**

Preheat oven to 375°F. Spray 12 muffin cups with nonstick cooking spray; set aside.

Combine plums, sugar, oil and egg until well blended. Combine flour, oat bran, baking soda, cinnamon and cloves in medium bowl. Stir into plum mixture just until moistened. Spoon evenly into prepared muffin cups.

Bake 20 minutes or until wooden pick inserted in center comes out clean. Cool in pan 5 minutes. Remove from pan. Cool on wire rack 10 minutes. Serve warm or cool completely.

*Makes 12 muffins*

*Favorite recipe from* **California Tree Fruit Agreement**

## QUINCE HAZELNUT MUFFINS

**2¼ cups granulated sugar**
**1¾ cups butter (softened)**
**1¼ cups packed brown sugar**
**⅓ cup almond paste**
**7 eggs, lightly beaten**
**4 teaspoons vanilla**
**2 cups buttermilk**
**4 cups all-purpose flour, sifted**
**4 teaspoons baking powder**
**¾ teaspoon baking soda**
**½ teaspoon salt**
**1 cup SMUCKER'S® Quince Jelly**
**½ cup ground hazelnuts**

Preheat oven to 350°F. Grease muffin cups; set aside. Beat granulated sugar, butter, brown sugar and almond paste in large bowl until light and fluffy. Stir in eggs just until mixed. Stir in vanilla and buttermilk. Combine flour, baking powder, baking soda and salt until well blended. Add to sugar mixture. Stir **Smucker's® Quince Jelly** and hazelnuts into sugar mixture just until moistened. Spoon evenly into prepared muffin cups. Bake 20 minutes or until wooden pick inserted in center comes out clean. Remove from pans. Cool on wire racks 10 minutes. Serve warm or cool completely.

*Makes 24 muffins*

*Spicy Plum Muffins*

SNACKIN' TREATS

## WHITE CHOCOLATE CHUNK MUFFINS

2½ **cups all-purpose flour**
1 **cup packed brown sugar**
⅓ **cup unsweetened cocoa powder**
2 **teaspoons baking soda**
½ **teaspoon salt**
1⅓ **cups buttermilk**
6 **tablespoons butter or margarine, melted**
2 **eggs, beaten**
1½ **teaspoons vanilla**
1½ **cups chopped white chocolate**

Preheat oven to 400°F. Grease 12 (3½-inch) large muffin cups; set aside.

Combine flour, sugar, cocoa, baking soda and salt in large bowl. Combine buttermilk, butter, eggs and vanilla in small bowl until blended. Stir into flour mixture just until moistened. Fold in white chocolate. Spoon into prepared muffin cups, filling half full.

Bake 25 to 30 minutes or until wooden pick inserted in center comes out clean. Cool in pan on wire rack 5 minutes. Remove from pan. Cool on wire rack 10 minutes. Serve warm or cool completely. *Makes 12 jumbo muffins*

## TOFFEE CRUNCH MUFFINS

1½ **cups all-purpose flour**
⅓ **cup packed brown sugar**
2 **teaspoons baking powder**
½ **teaspoon baking soda**
½ **teaspoon salt**
½ **cup milk**
½ **cup sour cream**
3 **tablespoons butter or margarine, melted**
1 **egg, beaten**
1 **teaspoon vanilla**
3 **bars (1.4 ounces each) chocolate-covered toffee, chopped and divided**

Preheat oven to 400°F. Grease or paper-line 36 (1¾-inch) mini-muffin cups; set aside.

Combine flour, sugar, baking powder, baking soda and salt in large bowl. Combine milk, sour cream, butter, egg and vanilla in small bowl until well blended. Stir into flour mixture just until moistened. Fold in two-thirds of toffee. Spoon into prepared muffin cups, filling almost full. Sprinkle remaining toffee evenly over tops of muffins.

Bake 16 to 18 minutes or until wooden pick inserted in center comes out clean. Remove from pans. Cool on wire racks 10 minutes. Serve warm or cool completely. *Makes 36 mini muffins*

*White Chocolate Chunk Muffins*

## SNACKIN' TREATS

## WILD RICE AND CARROT MUFFINS

¾ **cup all-purpose flour**
¾ **cup whole wheat flour**
½ **cup packed brown sugar**
2 **teaspoons baking powder**
1 **teaspoon ground cinnamon**
½ **teaspoon salt**
½ **teaspoon ground nutmeg**
2 **cups cooked wild rice (½ cup uncooked)**
¾ **cup milk**
⅓ **cup vegetable oil**
1 **egg, lightly beaten**
1 **cup shredded carrots**

**TOPPING**
1 **tablespoon granulated sugar**
¼ **teaspoon ground cinnamon**
  **Frosting (recipe follows)**

Preheat oven to 400°F. Grease or paper-line 12 muffin cups; set aside.

Combine flours, brown sugar, baking powder, 1 teaspoon cinnamon, salt and nutmeg in large bowl. Add wild rice to flour mixture; toss to coat.

Combine milk, oil and egg in medium bowl; add carrots. Stir into flour mixture just until moistened. Spoon evenly into prepared muffin cups.

For topping, combine granulated sugar and cinnamon; sprinkle over top of each muffin. Bake 25 to 30 minutes or until wooden pick inserted in

center comes out clean. Remove from pan. Cool on wire rack 10 minutes. Spoon Frosting over top of each muffin Serve warm or cool completely.

*Makes 12 muffins*

**FROSTING:** Combine 1 package (3 ounces) cream cheese, softened, and 1 cup sifted powdered sugar in medium bowl; blend until smooth.

*Favorite recipe from **Minnesota Cultivated Wild Rice Council***

## MOTT'S® GARDEN BOUNTY MUFFINS

1 **cup sugar**
1 **cup shredded zucchini**
1 **cup shredded carrots**
½ **cup raisins**
½ **cup MOTT'S® Natural Apple Sauce**
1 **egg**
2 **egg whites**
2 **tablespoons vegetable oil**
1 **teaspoon vanilla extract**
2 **cups all-purpose flour**
2 **teaspoons baking powder**
1 **teaspoon salt**
1 **teaspoon grated orange peel**
1 **teaspoon ground nutmeg**
½ **teaspoon baking soda**

**1.** Preheat oven to 400°F. Spray 12-cup muffin pan with nonstick cooking spray or paper-line; set aside.

# SNACKIN' TREATS

**2.** In large bowl, combine sugar, zucchini, carrots, raisins, apple sauce, egg, egg whites, oil and vanilla extract until well blended.

**3.** In medium bowl, combine flour, baking powder, salt, orange peel, nutmeg and baking soda.

**4.** Stir flour mixture into apple sauce mixture just until moistened.

**5.** Fill muffin cups ¾ full.

**6.** *Decrease oven temperature to 375°F.* Bake 25 to 30 minutes or until wooden pick inserted in center comes out clean. Remove from pan. Cool on wire rack 10 minutes. Serve warm or cool completely.

*Makes 12 muffins*

## BLUEBERRY-PLUM STREUSEL MUFFINS

**STREUSEL TOPPING**
   ¼ **cup all-purpose flour**
   ¼ **cup packed brown sugar**
   ¼ **cup margarine or butter, softened**
   ¼ **cup chopped nuts**
   1 **teaspoon cinnamon**

**MUFFINS**
   1 **egg**
   ½ **cup low fat milk**
   1 **packages (13 ounces) blueberry muffin mix**
   3 **fresh California plums, chopped (1 cup)**

Preheat oven to 375°F. Spray 12 muffin cups with nonstick cooking spray; set aside.

In small bowl, combine all topping ingredients; set aside. Combine egg and milk in medium bowl until well blended; stir in muffin mix just until moistened. Drain and rinse blueberries. Fold blueberries and plums into batter. Spoon evenly into prepared muffin cups. Sprinkle Streusel Topping over top of each muffin.

Bake 20 minutes or until wooden pick inserted in center comes out clean. Cool in pan 5 minutes. Remove from pan. Cool on wire rack 10 minutes. Serve warm or cool completely.

*Makes 12 muffins*

*Favorite recipe from* **California Tree Fruit Agreement**

# Acknowledgments

**The publisher would like to thank the companies and organizations listed below for the use of their recipes and photographs in this publication.**

Blue Diamond Growers

California Apricot Advisory Board

California Table Grape Commission

California Tree Fruit Agreement

Canned Food Information Council

Canned Fruit Promotion Service, Inc.

Del Monte Corporation

Florida Tomato Committee

Kraft Foods, Inc.

Thomas J. Lipton Co.

McIlhenny Company

Minnesota Cultivated Wild Rice Council

MOTT'S® U.S.A., a division of Cadbury Beverages Inc.

Nabisco Foods Group

National Dairy Board

National Honey Board

Nestlé Food Company

Oregon Washington California Pear Bureau

Pecan Marketing Board

Pet Incorporated

The Procter & Gamble Company

The Quaker Oats Company

The J.M. Smucker Company

The Sugar Association, Inc.

USA Dry Pea & Lentil Council

Washington Apple Commission

# Index

**A**
Almond Banana Bread, 24
Almond Blueberry Muffins, 10
Almond Brioches, 96
Anadama Bread, 50
Anjou Pear Cheese Muffins, 52
Apple & Raisin Scones, 68
Apple Butter Spice Muffins, 8
Apple Cheddar Scones, 66
Apple Oat Bran Muffins, 88
Apple Ring Coffee Cake, 28
Apple Sauce Cinnamon Rolls, 76
**Apples**
  Apple & Raisin Scones, 68
  Apple Butter Spice Muffins, 8
  Apple Cheddar Scones, 66
  Apple Oat Bran Muffins, 88
  Apple Ring Coffee Cake, 28
  Apple Sauce Cinnamon Rolls, 76
  Apple Saucy Oatmeal-Raisin Loaf or
    Muffins, 32
  Blueberry Muffins, 84
  Cinnamon Apple Tea Bread, 110
  Golden Apple Cheese Muffins, 12
  Golden Apple Sour Cream Muffins, 106
  Mott's® Best Ever Strawberry Muffins, 74
  Mott's® Garden Bounty Muffins, 122
  Mott's® Luscious Lemon Lite Muffins, 81
  Oatmeal Apple Cranberry Scones, 82
Apricot Nut Bread, 33
Apricot Scones, 16

**B**
Baked Doughnuts with Cinnamon Glaze,
  100
**Bananas**
  Almond Banana Bread, 24
  Banana Breakfast Muffins, 28
  Banana-Honey Muffins, 18
  Banana Nut Bread, 84
  Healthy Banana-Walnut Muffins, 30
  Mini Muffins, 91
  Sesame Crunch Banana Muffins, 78
**Biscuits**
  Chive Whole Wheat Drop Biscuits, 90
  Country Biscuits, 6
  Drop Biscuits, 58

  Herb-Cheese Biscuit Loaf, 46
  Rolled Biscuits, 58
  Sweet Heartland Biscuits, 25
  Sweet Potato Biscuits, 40
  Swiss Caraway Bread or Biscuits, 58
  Wild Rice Cheesy Biscuits, 50
**Blueberries**
  Almond Blueberry Muffins, 10
  Blueberry Crunch Muffins, 90
  Blueberry Muffins, 84
  Blueberry-Plum Streusel Muffins, 123
  Blueberry Yogurt Muffins, 72
  Streusel-Topped Blueberry Muffins, 98
  Wild Rice and Blueberry Muffins, 24
  Wild Rice Blueberry Muffins, 86
**Buttermilk**
  Apple Oat Bran Muffins, 88
  Apricot Nut Bread, 33
  Buttermilk Oatmeal Scones, 8
  Healthy Banana-Walnut Muffins, 30
  Irish Soda Bread, 104
  Mott's® Best Ever Strawberry Muffins,
    74
  Peanut Butter Mini Chip Loaves, 114
  Pear Scones, 80
  Pumpkin Pecan Nut Bread, 116
  Pumpkin Pecan Nut Muffins, 116
  Quick Nectarine Oat Muffins, 94
  Quince Hazelnut Muffins, 118
  Spanish Olive Cheddar Muffins, 69
  Sun-Dried Tomato 'n' Cheese Muffins,
    68
  Sweet Heartland Biscuits, 25
  White Chocolate Chunk Muffins, 120

**C**
Caraway Cheese Muffins, 60
Carrot Zucchini Muffins, 80
Cheddar Cheese Pepper Bread, 58
**Cheese**
  Anjou Pear Cheese Muffins, 52
  Apple Cheddar Scones, 66
  Caraway Cheese Muffins, 60
  Cheddar Cheese Pepper Bread, 58
  Cheese and Nut Scones, 44
  Cherry Coconut Cheese Coffee Cake, 26
  Chive Whole Wheat Drop Biscuits, 90

  Cornmeal Sticks, 38
  Drop Biscuits, 58
  Feta-Dill Muffins, 46
  Frosting, 122
  Golden Apple Cheese Muffins, 12
  Herb and Cheddar Scones, 44
  Herb-Cheese Biscuit Loaf, 46
  Parmesan Cheese Scones, 69
  Parmesan Garlic Twists, 45
  Pesto Surprise Muffins, 44
  Rolled Biscuits, 58
  Spanish Olive Cheddar Muffins, 69
  Sun-Dried Tomato 'n' Cheese Muffins,
    68
  Swiss Caraway Bread or Biscuits, 58
  Tabasco® Corn Bread Wedges, 57
  Thyme-Cheese Bubble Loaf, 36
  Wild Rice Cheesy Biscuits, 50
  Zucchini Cheese Muffins, 62
Cherry Coconut Cheese Coffee Cake, 26
Chive Whole Wheat Drop Biscuits, 90
**Chocolate**
  Chocolate Popovers, 116
  Chocolate Pumpkin Muffins, 102
  German Chocolate Muffins, 111
  German Chocolate Topping, 111
  Mini Crumbcakes, 112
  Mint Chocolate Chip Muffins, 98
  Oreo® Muffins, 114
  Peanut Butter Mini Chip Loaves, 114
  Topping, 112
  White Chocolate Chunk Muffins, 120
**Cinnamon**
  Apple Sauce Cinnamon Rolls, 76
  Apple Saucy Oatmeal-Raisin Loaf or
    Muffins, 32
  Baked Doughnuts with Cinnamon Glaze,
    100
  Cinnamon Apple Tea Bread, 110
  Cinnamon Buns, 10
  Cinnamon-Date Scones, 18
  Cinnamon-Raisin Bread, 108
Cloverleaf Rolls, 56
**Coffee Cakes**
  Apple Ring Coffee Cake, 28
  Cherry Coconut Cheese Coffee Cake, 26
  Maple Nut Twist, 22

**Cornmeal**
Anadama Bread, 50
Cornmeal Sticks, 38
Indian Corn Muffins, 70
Salsa Muffins, 38
Tabasco® Corn Bread Wedges, 57
Country Biscuits, 6
Cranberry Oat Bran Muffins, 88
Crescent Rolls, 56
Crunch Topping, 91

**D**
Dilled Popovers, 40
Dill Sour Cream Scones, 62
Dinner Rolls, 56
Drop Biscuits, 58

**F**
Fan-Tan Rolls, 57
Feta-Dill Muffins, 46
Five-Fruit Granola Scones, 20
freezing muffins, 13, 30, 52, 81
French Bread, 48
Fresh Nectarine Muffins, 16
Frosting, 122

**G**
German Chocolate Muffins, 111
German Chocolate Topping, 111
Gingerbread Pear Muffins, 94
Glazed Strawberry Lemon Streusel Muffins, 106
Golden Apple Cheese Muffins, 12
Golden Apple Sour Cream Muffins, 106
Graham Muffins, 26

**H**
Healthy Banana-Walnut Muffins, 30
Herb and Cheddar Scones, 44
Herb-Cheese Biscuit Loaf, 46
Honey Currant Scones, 30
Honey Muffins, 102
Honey-Mustard Scones, 52
Honey Shortbread, 104
Hot Cross Buns, 14

**I**
Indian Corn Muffins, 70
In-the-Chips Carrot Muffins, 110
Irish Soda Bread, 104

**K**
kneading dough, 13

**L**
Lemon Poppy Seed Muffins, 112
Lemon Streusel Topping, 106
Lemony Glaze, 106

**M**
Maple Nut Twist, 22
Marble Swirl Bread, 54
Mini Crumbcakes, 112
Mini Muffins, 91
Mint Chocolate Chip Muffins, 98
Mott's® Best Ever Strawberry Muffins, 74
Mott's® Garden Bounty Muffins, 122
Mott's® Luscious Lemon Lite Muffins, 81
**Muffins**
Almond Blueberry Muffins, 10
Anjou Pear Cheese Muffins, 52
Apple Butter Spice Muffins, 8
Apple Oat Bran Muffins, 88
Apple Saucy Oatmeal-Raisin Loaf or Muffins, 32
Banana Breakfast Muffins, 28
Banana-Honey Muffins, 18
Blueberry Crunch Muffins, 90
Blueberry Muffins, 84
Blueberry-Plum Streusel Muffins, 123
Blueberry Yogurt Muffins, 72
Caraway Cheese Muffins, 60
Carrot Zucchini Muffins, 80
Chocolate Pumpkin Muffins, 102
Cranberry Oat Bran Muffins, 88
Feta-Dill Muffins, 46
Fresh Nectarine Muffins, 16
German Chocolate Muffins, 111
Gingerbread Pear Muffins, 94
Glazed Strawberry Lemon Streusel Muffins, 106
Golden Apple Cheese Muffins, 12
Golden Apple Sour Cream Muffins, 106
Graham Muffins, 26
Healthy Banana-Walnut Muffins, 30
Honey Muffins, 102
Indian Corn Muffins, 70
In-the-Chips Carrot Muffins, 110
Lemon Poppy Seed Muffins, 112
Mini Muffins, 91
Mint Chocolate Chip Muffins, 98
Mott's® Best Ever Strawberry Muffins, 74
Mott's® Garden Bounty Muffins, 122
Mott's® Luscious Lemon Lite Muffins, 81
Nectarine Bran Muffins, 33
Nectarine Pecan Breakfast Muffins, 25
Newton Muffins, 92
Orange-Almond Muffins, 10

Oreo® Muffins, 114
Pesto Surprise Muffins, 44
Pineapple-Raisin Muffins, 20
Pumpkin Pecan Nut Muffins, 116
Quick Nectarine Oat Muffins, 94
Quince Hazelnut Muffins, 118
Salsa Muffins, 38
Savory Pumpkin Bacon Muffins, 57
Sesame Crunch Banana Muffins, 78
Spanish Olive Cheddar Muffins, 69
Spicy Plum Muffins, 118
Squash Muffins, 60
Streusel-Topped Blueberry Muffins, 98
Sun-Dried Tomato 'n' Cheese Muffins, 68
Toffee Crunch Muffins, 120
White Chocolate Chunk Muffins, 120
Wild Rice and Blueberry Muffins, 24
Wild Rice and Carrot Muffins, 122
Wild Rice Blueberry Muffins, 86
Zucchini Cheese Muffins, 62

**N**
Nectarine Bran Muffins, 33
Nectarine Pecan Breakfast Muffins, 25
Newton Muffins, 92
**Nuts**
Almond Banana Bread, 24
Almond Blueberry Muffins, 10
Almond Brioches, 96
Anjou Pear Cheese Muffins, 52
Apple Butter Spice Muffins, 8
Apple Ring Coffee Cake, 28
Apricot Nut Bread, 33
Banana Nut Bread, 84
Cheese and Nut Scones, 44
Cinnamon Apple Tea Bread, 110
Healthy Banana-Walnut Muffins, 30
Honey Shortbread, 104
Maple Nut Twist, 22
Nectarine Pecan Breakfast Muffins, 25
Orange-Almond Muffins, 10
Pumpkin Pecan Nut Bread, 116
Pumpkin Pecan Nut Muffins, 116
Quince Hazelnut Muffins, 118
Sweet Potato Biscuits, 40
Topping, 112

**O**
**Oats**
Apple Saucy Oatmeal-Raisin Loaf or Muffins, 32
Buttermilk Oatmeal Scones, 8
Carrot Zucchini Muffins, 80
Mott's® Luscious Lemon Lite Muffins, 81

Oatmeal Apple Cranberry Scones, 82
Plum Oat Squares, 111
Quick Nectarine Oat Muffins, 94
Sesame Crunch Banana Muffins, 78
Sweet Heartland Biscuits, 25
Orange-Almond Muffins, 10
Oreo® Muffins, 114

**P**
Parmesan Cheese Scones, 69
Parmesan Garlic Twists, 45
Peach Spread, 91
Peanut Butter Mini Chip Loaves, 114
Pear Scones, 80
Pesto Surprise Muffins, 44
Pineapple-Raisin Muffins, 20
Plum Oat Squares, 111
Pumpkin-Ginger Scones, 70
Pumpkin Pecan Nut Bread, 116
Pumpkin Pecan Nut Muffins, 116

**Q**
**Quick Loaves**
  Almond Banana Bread, 24
  Apple Saucy Oatmeal-Raisin Loaf or
    Muffins, 32
  Apricot Nut Bread, 33
  Banana Nut Bread, 84
  Cheddar Cheese Pepper Bread, 58
  Cinnamon Apple Tea Bread, 110
  Herb-Cheese Biscuit Loaf, 46
  Irish Soda Bread, 104
  Peanut Butter Mini Chip Loaves, 114
  Pumpkin Pecan Nut Bread, 116
  Spice-Prune Loaf, 86
  Swiss Caraway Bread or Biscuits, 58
Quick Nectarine Oat Muffins, 94
Quince Hazelnut Muffins, 118

**R**
**Raisins**
  Apple & Raisin Scones, 68
  Apple Saucy Oatmeal-Raisin Loaf or
    Muffins, 32
  Banana Breakfast Muffins, 28
  Cinnamon Apple Tea Bread, 110
  Cinnamon-Raisin Bread, 108
  Fresh Nectarine Muffins, 16
  Golden Apple Sour Cream Muffins,
    106
  Hot Cross Buns, 14
  Irish Soda Bread, 104
  Mott's® Garden Bounty Muffins, 122
  Mott's® Luscious Lemon Lite Muffins, 81

Pineapple-Raisin Muffins, 20
Squash Muffins, 60
Raisin Scones, 44
Roasted Garlic Bread Sticks, 64
Rolled Biscuits, 58
**Rye Flour**
  Caraway Cheese Muffins, 60
  Marble Swirl Bread, 54
  Rye Bread, 42

**S**
Salsa Muffins, 38
Savory Pumpkin Bacon Muffins, 57
**Scones**
  Apple & Raisin Scones, 68
  Apple Cheddar Scones, 66
  Apricot Scones, 16
  Buttermilk Oatmeal Scones, 8
  Cheese and Nut Scones, 44
  Cinnamon-Date Scones, 18
  Dill Sour Cream Scones, 62
  Five-Fruit Granola Scones, 20
  Herb and Cheddar Scones, 44
  Honey Currant Scones, 30
  Honey-Mustard Scones, 52
  Oatmeal Apple Cranberry Scones, 82
  Parmesan Cheese Scones, 69
  Pear Scones, 80
  Pumpkin-Ginger Scones, 70
  Raisin Scones, 44
  Scones, 44
  Wheat Germ Scones, 13
Sesame Crunch Banana Muffins, 78
Sesame Crunch Topping, 78
Spanish Olive Cheddar Muffins, 69
Spice-Prune Loaf, 86
Spicy Plum Muffins, 118
Squash Muffins, 60
Streusel-Topped Blueberry Muffins, 98
Sun-Dried Tomato 'n' Cheese Muffins, 68
Sweet Heartland Biscuits, 25
Sweet Potato Biscuits, 40
Sweet Yeast Dough, 12
Swiss Caraway Bread or Biscuits, 58

**T**
Tabasco® Corn Bread Wedges, 57
Thyme-Cheese Bubble Loaf, 36
Toffee Crunch Muffins, 120
Tomato-Carrot Muffin Tops, 66
**Toppings**
  Crunch Topping, 91
  German Chocolate Topping, 111
  Lemon Streusel Topping, 106

Lemony Glaze, 106
Peach Spread, 91
Sesame Crunch Topping, 78
Topping, 112

**W**
Wheat Germ Scones, 13
White Chocolate Chunk Muffins, 120
**Whole Wheat Flour**
  Apple Oat Bran Muffins, 88
  Blueberry Crunch Muffins, 90
  Chive Whole Wheat Drop Biscuits,
    90
  Mini Muffins, 91
  Nectarine Pecan Breakfast Muffins, 25
  Pear Scones, 80
  Quick Nectarine Oat Muffins, 94
  Sesame Crunch Banana Muffins, 78
  Spice-Prune Loaf, 86
  Squash Muffins, 60
  Whole Wheat Herb Bread, 74
  Whole Wheat Popovers, 34
  Wild Rice and Carrot Muffins, 122
Whole Wheat Popovers, 34
Wild Rice and Blueberry Muffins, 24
Wild Rice and Carrot Muffins, 122
Wild Rice Blueberry Muffins, 86
Wild Rice Cheesy Biscuits, 50

**Y**
**Yeast Breads**
  Almond Brioches, 96
  Anadama Bread, 50
  Apple Sauce Cinnamon Rolls, 76
  Baked Doughnuts with Cinnamon Glaze,
    100
  Cinnamon Buns, 10
  Cinnamon-Raisin Bread, 108
  Cloverleaf Rolls, 56
  Crescent Rolls, 56
  Dinner Rolls, 56
  Fan-Tan Rolls, 57
  French Bread, 48
  Hot Cross Buns, 14
  Maple Nut Twist, 22
  Marble Swirl Bread, 54
  Roasted Garlic Bread Sticks, 64
  Rye Bread, 42
  Sweet Yeast Dough, 12
  Thyme-Cheese Bubble Loaf, 36
  Whole Wheat Herb Bread, 74

**Z**
Zucchini Cheese Muffins, 62

# METRIC CONVERSION CHART

## VOLUME MEASUREMENTS (dry)

⅛ teaspoon = 0.5 mL
¼ teaspoon = 1 mL
½ teaspoon = 2 mL
¾ teaspoon = 4 mL
1 teaspoon = 5 mL
1 tablespoon = 15 mL
2 tablespoons = 30 mL
¼ cup = 60 mL
⅓ cup = 75 mL
½ cup = 125 mL
⅔ cup = 150 mL
¾ cup = 175 mL
1 cup = 250 mL
2 cups = 1 pint = 500 mL
3 cups = 750 mL
4 cups = 1 quart = 1 L

## VOLUME MEASUREMENTS (fluid)

1 fluid ounce (2 tablespoons) = 30 mL
4 fluid ounces (½ cup) = 125 mL
8 fluid ounces (1 cup) = 250 mL
12 fluid ounces (1½ cups) = 375 mL
16 fluid ounces (2 cups) = 500 mL

## WEIGHTS (mass)

½ ounce = 15 g
1 ounce = 30 g
3 ounces = 90 g
4 ounces = 120 g
8 ounces = 225 g
10 ounces = 285 g
12 ounces = 360 g
16 ounces = 1 pound = 450 g

## DIMENSIONS

1/16 inch = 2 mm
⅛ inch = 3 mm
¼ inch = 6 mm
½ inch = 1.5 cm
¾ inch = 2 cm
1 inch = 2.5 cm

## OVEN TEMPERATURES

250°F = 120°C
275°F = 140°C
300°F = 150°C
325°F = 160°C
350°F = 180°C
375°F = 190°C
400°F = 200°C
425°F = 220°C
450°F = 230°C

## BAKING PAN SIZES

| Utensil | Size in Inches/Quarts | Metric Volume | Size in Centimeters |
|---|---|---|---|
| Baking or Cake Pan (square or rectangular) | 8×8×2 | 2 L | 20×20×5 |
| | 9×9×2 | 2.5 L | 22×22×5 |
| | 12×8×2 | 3 L | 30×20×5 |
| | 13×9×2 | 3.5 L | 33×23×5 |
| Loaf Pan | 8×4×3 | 1.5 L | 20×10×7 |
| | 9×5×3 | 2 L | 23×13×7 |
| Round Layer Cake Pan | 8×1½ | 1.2 L | 20×4 |
| | 9×1½ | 1.5 L | 23×4 |
| Pie Plate | 8×1¼ | 750 mL | 20×3 |
| | 9×1¼ | 1 L | 23×3 |
| Baking Dish or Casserole | 1 quart | 1 L | — |
| | 1½ quart | 1.5 L | — |
| | 2 quart | 2 L | — |